NEW WINE

20 12/07 on 10/15 keep

NANZAN STUDIES IN ASIAN RELIGIONS
Paul L. Swanson, General Editor

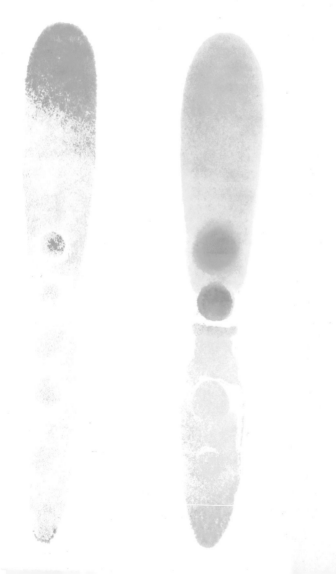

NEW WINE

The Cultural Shaping
of Japanese Christianity   CCL

David Reid

ASIAN HUMANITIES PRESS
Berkeley, California

ASIAN HUMANITIES PRESS

Asian Humanities Press offers to the specialist and the general reader alike the best in new translations of major works and significant original contributions to our understanding of Asian religions, cultures and thought.

Acknowledgments

The author and the Nanzan Institute for Religion and Culture wish to express their thanks to Japan Ecumenical Books for assisting in the publication of this book and to the Niwano Peace Foundation for the award of a Grant in Aid.

Photo credits: Photo 1 of Yasukuni Shrine on p. 51 by George Pope; photos 2–4 on pp. 127–28 by Kasugai Shin'ei; photo 5 on p. 134 by Kawakami Michiyo.

Printed in the United States of America

Library of Congress Cataloging-in-Publication Data

Reid, David (1927–)
    New wine: the cultural shaping of Japanese Christianity / David Reid.
      p.   cm. — (Nanzan studies in Asian religions ; 2)
    Includes bibliographical references and index.
    ISBN 0-89581-931-7 (cloth). — ISBN 0-89581-932-5 (pbk.)
    1. Christianity—Japan—History. 2. Christianity and culture. 3. Japan—Religion—History. 4. Ancestor worship—Christianity. 5. Religion and state—Japan. I. Title. II. Series.
BR1305.R375   1991
275.2—dc20
                                                                91-7732
                                                                CIP

Contents

Preface

Forty momentous years have passed since 1950 when I first came to Japan. Now I am on the verge of retirement. Yet inwardly, I feel much as I did in my twenties, as if I were just getting started.

This book stands at the end of a career. It marks, however, not so much an end as a beginning. I shall explain in a moment the sense in which this is true. But first I had better say a word about the title and overall plan of the book.

The main title comes from words attributed to Jesus in Luke 5:36–39:

> No one tears a piece from a new cloak to patch an old one; if he does, he will have made a hole in the new cloak, and the patch from the new will not match the old. Nor does anyone put new wine into old wine-skins; if he does, the new wine will burst the skins, the wine will be wasted, and the skins ruined. Fresh skins for new wine! And no one after drinking old wine wants new; for he says, "The old wine is good."

In the Japanese context, the Christian message is the new wine. For many it makes life convivial and exuberant. But there are others who understandably prefer "the old wine," the traditional virtues and accepted ways of being human in Japan. The main title is at once an explicit reference to Christianity and an implicit reference to the Japanese milieu.

One of the chief interests of this book is to understand how a religion changes as it moves from one culture to another. The subtitle, "The Cultural Shaping of Japanese Christianity," pinpoints this interest. Part 1, "A Bird's-eye View," sets the stage for part 2, "Studies in Japanese Christianity."

The last chapter, "Japanese Christians and the Ancestors,"

was written with a sense of discovery. So far as I know, this is the first time that anyone has divided Japanese Christians and non-Christians into groups with an ancestral altar in the home and groups without such an altar in the home—and then compared them as to beliefs and practices. The results must speak for themselves, but the point I want to note here is that I have only begun to scratch the surface of this important topic. There is an immense amount of research that needs to be accomplished before we can obtain a complete picture. In this sense the book marks not an end but a beginning.

With the exception of the chapter on religion and state, which is new, this book represents a distillation of previously published writings. Chapter 1, "Japanese Religions," is reproduced in revised form by permission of Penguin Books Ltd from *A Handbook of Living Religions* edited by John R. Hinnells (Harmondsworth, Middlesex, England: Viking, 1984), 365–91. (Illustrations, maps and diagrams by Raymond Thurvey. Copyright © Penguin Books Ltd, 1984.)

Chapter 2, in its first incarnation, was coauthored with the late Professor Yanagawa under the title "Between Unity and Separation: Religion and Politics in Japan, 1965–1977." It appeared in the *Japanese Journal of Religious Studies* 6 (1979). Originally written to examine what secularization might mean if applied to a postwar series of events, it has been rewritten not to test a theory but to identify a trend.

Chapters 3–6 all made their first appearance in the *Japanese Journal of Religious Studies*: chapter 3 in volume 13 (1986), chapter 4 in volume 6 (1979), chapter 5 in volume 8 (1981), and chapter 6 in volume 16 (1989). They are reproduced here with varying degrees of revision by kind permission of the International Institute for the Study of Religions and the Nanzan Institute for Religion and Culture.

This book would never have seen the light of day had it not been for three people, now deceased. One is my father, James Dee Reid (1905–1973). His Christmas gift of a thesaurus in 1945 was my first introduction to the tortuous pleasure of finding the right word. I am still using it. The second is Dr. Lowell B. Hazzard (1898–1978), my teacher both at Illinois Wesleyan University and at Wesley Theological Seminary. It was he who brought home to me the universality of the Christian message and thus made me inwardly ready to hear a call to serve as a missionary in Japan. The third is Professor Yanagawa Keiichi (1926–1990), my mentor in the University of Tokyo Graduate School. When I had tired of studying abstract Buddhist doctrines and wanted to learn more about the actual religious life of contemporary Japanese people, it was he who encouraged and guided me. I shall always be in his debt.

I want to express a special word of thanks to David L. Swain, Director of Japan Ecumenical Books, a fellow writer, translator, and editor, and a close friend for nearly forty years, for scrutinizing every page of the first draft and writing marginal notes to call my attention to errors, stylistic infelicities, and non sequiturs. Responsibility for the text as it stands is of course my own, but because of the care and expertise he has lavished on this book, my confidence in presenting it to the reading public has been immeasurably strengthened.

I am also deeply grateful to Paul L. Swanson and James Heisig of the Nanzan Institute for Religion and Culture, who not only encouraged the idea of publishing this book in the Nanzan Studies in Asian Religions series, but also put their editorial experience and computer skills to work on the disk I sent them and prepared camera-ready copy, complete with an index, for the Asian Humanities Press.

Finally, I want to express appreciation to my wife, Etsu, whose encouragement was consistent and sustaining even when she thought I was just "playing" at the computer, and to my mother, Theodosia Kinyon Reid, whose impatience with my slow writing pace probably did not interfere too much with the production of this book.

David Reid

Linguistic Conventions

Throughout this book, Japanese names are presented in the order customary in Japan: first the family name, then the personal name. For "Yanagawa Keiichi," accordingly, the proper abbreviated reference is not "Keiichi" but "Yanagawa." In the bibliography, the family names of authors and editors (not translators) appear in small caps (e.g., YANAGAWA). The index gives all family names in small caps.

In the case of premodern historical figures known by a single name, however, the name is presented in lower case letters, as in Saichō, Kūkai, Nichiren, and the like.

In principle, the Japanese syllable ん is regularly transliterated by n. This eliminates the complicated rule of changing n to m before b, m, and p, the norm for spoken Japanese. The Tokyo district of 新橋 , consequently, is written *Shinbashi* (rather than *Shimbashi*). But in the case of a proper noun where m is the specified written standard, as in *Yomiuri Shimbun*, the older form is retained.

Part 1

A Bird's-eye View

Chapter 1

Japanese Religions

RELIGION IS OFTEN STUDIED as if personal faith were the key thing and all else mere appendage. This approach is not always possible in Japan, where religious phenomena include many dimensions to which faith is irrelevant. Shinto festivals and Buddhist mortuary rites, for example, are not commonly thought of as part of personal religion. Some sects, moreover, place no emphasis whatever on faith, preferring a "try-it-and-see" attitude. Nonetheless, there are also areas where personal belief is essential, as in the great majority of sects.

One thing that these disparate religious phenomena have in common is behavior. In this discussion, behavior will be considered "religious" if it expresses a relationship with a divine being or beings, as in Shinto, popular Buddhism, Christianity, and folk religion, or with a life-transforming principle at once ultimate and immanent, as in elite forms of Buddhism.

Living religion in Japan, as elsewhere, includes an organizational dimension. Religious organizations have their own internal histories, to be sure; but for the student of Japanese religion and society, more significant is the question of the changing relationships between religious organizations and the state. Throughout most Japanese history, the state has set the terms within which such organizations could exist. It is important, therefore, to give a brief account of the continuing interplay between these two life-shaping influences: religious organizations and state power.

RELIGIOUS STUDIES IN JAPAN

Broadly construed, the term "religious studies" as used in Japan includes every academic discipline that takes religion as its object of study. Narrowly construed, the term excludes not only theological and philosophical studies but also historical and textual studies. It is limited to disciplines in which contemporary religious phenomena are studied empirically and, at least in principle, comparatively. Phenomenology of religion, anthropology of religion, psychology of religion, and sociology of religion constitute the principal disciplines.

THE "COSMIC RELIGION" MATRIX

Scholars of the world's religions have employed numerous concepts in order to distinguish types of religion. Dissatisfaction with one set of concepts has repeatedly led to new proposals, and frequently the motive power for a new proposal is moral. "Primitive religions," a term once in wide use for the religions of preliterate societies, has been abandoned by many because of the disparagement that some associate with the word "primitive." One term proposed as a substitute is "primal religions" or "the religions of primal societies." Again, following a suggestion made by the anthropologist Robert Redfield, it has become customary to distinguish "great" traditions, characterized by highly developed systems of thought and doctrine, from "little" traditions, in which such systems appear less fully developed. Yet these terms too, contrary to Redfield's intention, often carry a value connotation offensive to people in the traditions categorized as "little." I propose, therefore, to adopt the recommendation of the Sri Lankan scholar Aloysius Pieris, who distinguishes between "cosmic" and "metacosmic" religions.[1] "Cosmic religion" has to do with powers intrinsic to this world: powers symbolized by water, fire, mountains, ancient trees, oddly shaped stones, the spirits of dead people, etc. "Metacosmic religion" has to do with a being or principle that transcends this

---

[1] Aloysius Pieris, *An Asian Theology of Liberation* (Maryknoll, New York: Orbis Books, 1988), 72 and frequently.

world: God, Allah, Brahma, Dharma, etc. On this basis, the term "cosmic religion" will be applied to Shinto in its three principal forms: folk Shinto, Shrine Shinto and Sect Shinto. The term "metacosmic religions" will refer to Japanese Buddhism and Christianity.

Shinto has a highly complex history of its own. It resists systematic portrayal. One may identify, however, two general tendencies in Japanese ways of thinking that have their roots in Shinto.

One deep-seated and far-reaching motif is the emphasis on Shinto as something that unifies. Ideally, its festivals unite people with the *kami*, divine beings more immanent than transcendent, who desire to see their people enjoying a life of communal harmony and abundance, filled with dynamic vitality and purity of heart. Socially, this unity is sought primarily at two levels: the local community and the national community. In both cases the expectation is that the oneness achieved, whether interpreted religiously or not, will lead to increasing productivity, creativity and prosperity.

In all this, the role of the emperor is central. For historical reasons to be touched on later, the emperor is the chief priest of the Shinto world. In modern Japan (from 1868 onward), he has also played a key role in the Japanese state. Together, these two roles helped shape the stubborn problem of the relationship between religion and state power. From 701 C. E., when the law of the land was first codified, until 1945, when defeat in war led to the institutionalization of the hitherto alien value of government neutrality in respect of religion, the dominant assumption was that religion was properly at the service of the state.[2] This centuries-old feature or tendency in "cosmic" religion strongly affected the way people perceived, evaluated, and modified the imported "metacosmic religions."

The other motif of Shinto thought to be considered here is the emphasis on different kinds of divinities or kami. Hori Ichirō

---

[2] Kawawata Yuiken, "Religious Organizations in Japanese Law" in Hori Ichirō et al., eds., *Japanese Religion: A Survey by the Agency for Cultural Affairs*, transl. by Abe Yoshiya and David Reid (Tokyo and Palo Alto: Kodansha International Ltd, 1972), 162.

distinguishes between two main types: clan kami and charismatic kami.[3] Clan kami, associated with rites for the ancestors, were initially the ritual focus of territorially limited and mutually exclusive quasi-genealogical bodies. Generally beneficent, kami of this type had no clearly defined personalities or functions. Charismatic kami, associated with local shrines, were originally objects of faith who united people from different social and regional groups. Such kami had sharply defined personalities and performed specific functions such as healing. Over the years, these two types became intertwined.

In modern Japan, Shrine Shinto can be viewed as a religion of clan kami in an enlarged, more comprehensive sense. The kami of local communities have their parishes, and the kami associated with the imperial household embrace the entire nation. In both cases they unite people in a sense that transcends the genealogical nexus. The charismatic kami come into view primarily in the new religious movements. These movements will receive consideration later, but here it should be emphasized that for centuries people with urgent personal problems have sought help from one charismatic kami or another, one shamanistic leader or another. Such practices and expectations have given rise to what is now a widespread tendency: to assume that religion oriented to a "living kami" should provide tangible, this-worldly benefits. This tendency too has guided people's perceptions, evaluations, and modifications of the imported "metacosmic religions."

RELIGIOUS TRADITIONS IN JAPANESE HISTORY

The story of the interaction between religious traditions and the state is a continuing one. In order to sketch this story, I propose to use the Ministry of Education classifications employed in the tabulation of statistical data concerning religious organizations:

---

[3] Hori Ichirō, *Folk Religion in Japan: Continuity and Change* (Chicago: University of Chicago Press; Tokyo: University of Tokyo Press, 1968), 30–34.

Shinto, Buddhist, Christian, and Other (see table 1).[4] I shall
divide this history into four periods representing cumulative
layers of religious tradition.

TABLE 1

ADHERENTS TO MAJOR CLASSES OF RELIGIOUS TRADITION

YEAR	TRADITION					POPULATION OF JAPAN
	Shinto	Buddhist	Christian	Other	Total	
1953	77,780,324	47,714,876	485,399	3,419,471	129,400,070	86,981,000
1958	76,844,827	48,974,838	652,518	4,010,745	130,482,928	91,767,000
1963	80,284,643	69,843,367	711,636	5,350,790	156,190,436	96,156,000
1968	83,458,684	83,278,496	831,335	6,768,042	174,336,557	101,331,000
1973	87,414,779	84,573,828	879,477	10,002,986	182,871,070	109,104,000
1978	98,545,703	88,020,880	950,491	13,729,376	201,246,450	115,190,000
1983	116,889,434	87,469,117	1,574,630	14,849,964	220,783,145	119,536,000
1988	111,791,562	93,109,006	1,422,858	11,377,217	217,700,643	122,783,000

SOURCES: Figures on adherents are taken from the Ministry of Education
Shūkyō nenkan [Religions yearbook] (Tokyo: Bunkachō). They represent the
numbers of people claimed by religious organizations as of December 31 in
a given year. The population figures, rounded off to the nearest thousand,
appear in the *Japan Statistical Yearbook* (Tokyo: Nihon Tōkei Kyōkai) and
represent the situation as of October 1 in a given year.

SHINTO PERIOD (PRE–SIXTH CENTURY)

The key development in the first period was the regionally
limited establishment, about the middle of the fourth century
C.E., of a hereditary priestly rule that, exceptions aside, contin-
ues to the present day in the imperial household. The religious
practices later given the name "Shinto" are closely tied to the
priestly role of the empresses and emperors in this line. These
practices, fundamentally concerned with food and the sun, involved priestly tasks not only for the chief ruler but also for the
heads of the many clans. The divine beings whose favor they
sought, the kami, were of many kinds: kami of nature, kami of
ideas, kami in outstanding people, ancestral kami, etc.[5] Two major

---

[4] The organizations found under "Other" are generally spoken of as "new religions," but the Shinto, Buddhist and Christian classifications also include some "new"
religious organizations. See table 2.
[5] Hirai Naofusa, "Shinto," *Encyclopaedia Britannica*, 15th ed., *Macropaedia* (Chicago: Encyclopaedia Britannica, 1982), 16: 672.

festivals were held, one in the spring to pray for a successful harvest, the other in the autumn to celebrate the harvest granted. Divination and purification were important features. The reigning empress or emperor, who had to observe many taboos, was regarded as possessing the mystical power to receive influences from the sun goddess, augment the food supply, and thereby protect the well-being of the people.

SHINTO-BUDDHIST PERIOD (538–1549)

In 538 (or 552 according to some scholars), when Buddhism was introduced from Korea, political control in Japan was not yet centralized. Clan heads were in effect the heads of village states. Imperial court control, though growing, was by no means complete. In this situation Buddhism was regarded in two completely different ways. The imperial court saw Buddhism as a way of promoting a spiritual outlook that would support with magico-religious power its claims to "universality." Village-state heads saw it as a threat to autonomy and tradition. Confucian morality, entering Japan in the fifth century together with the Chinese system of writing, weakly complemented Buddhism as an ordering of human relationships that strengthened the hand of male power-holders. Efforts to centralize political power included the development of official compilations of Shinto myth and legend, an endeavor that modern scholars interpret as a means of legitimizing the imperial house.

Between 538 and 1549, Buddhism took deeper root in successive waves of sectarian tradition (see graph 1). The Nara, Tendai, and Shingon sects were imported from China between the seventh and ninth centuries, when political power resided in the imperial court. The Pure Land, Zen, and Nichiren sects, more interested in winning believers among the masses, began just before and during the Kamakura period (1185–1333), when leading men of the military or samurai class were seizing political power and the emperor was sinking into obscurity. The changing relationships between Shinto and Buddhism reflect these political conditions. When power was held by the court, Buddhist thinkers, then in favor, accommodated Shinto to Buddhism. When power fell to the Kamakura military government,

Shinto thinkers, in reaction, accommodated Buddhism to Shinto. In time, the two became interwoven both doctrinally and institutionally.

SHINTO-BUDDHIST-CHRISTIAN PERIOD (1549–1802)

Christianity entered the scene in 1549. The shogunate (government under the shogun or leading general) was then at a low ebb. Fief heads or daimyo, relatively autonomous, warred with

GRAPH 1

LAYERS OF RELIGIOUS TRADITION

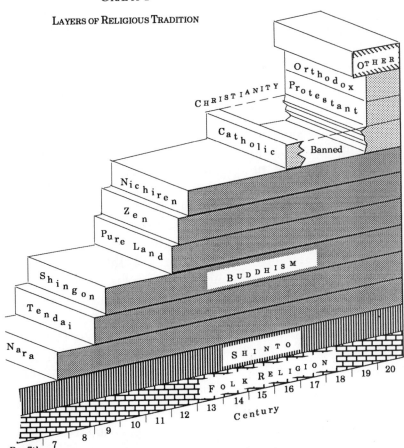

Note: Buddhism entered Japan from Korea in 538 (or 552) C.E., when Buddhist sutras, an image, and ritual paraphernalia were presented by the king of what was then Kudara to the emperor of Japan. Sect traditions began as shown.

one another to enlarge their domains. Tendai, Nichiren, and Pure Land soldier-monks armed themselves, fortified their monasteries and took sides in the fray. Under Oda Nobunaga (1534– 1582) order was restored in central Japan, but in the process, opposing monasteries were razed and thousands of monks killed. His successor, Toyotomi Hideyoshi (1536–1598), established a military dictatorship over the entire country. Christianity was outlawed in a series of inconsistently enforced edicts that began with Hideyoshi's expulsion of Catholic missionaries in 1587 and his crucifixion of twenty-six Japanese and foreign Christians in 1597. It grew under Tokugawa Ieyasu (1542–1616) to include the exiling of Japanese Christians to Manila and Macao in 1612, and the further executing of Christians under his son Hidetada (1578–1632). The opposition to Christianity culminated in an absolute prohibition following the abortive Shimabara Revolt of 1637–1638.

Buddhism was put into government service with the establishment of the *danka seido* (1638), a system that required every Japanese household to register with and financially support a local temple, and the *terauke seido* (1662), whereby every adult was required to obtain annually from this temple a certificate attesting that he or she was innocent of association with subversive religion, namely, Christianity. These developments led to the formation of underground Christian congregations – some of which persist today. Not surprisingly, mandatory ties to Buddhist temples, the only institutions then authorized to conduct mortuary rites, weakened voluntary interest in Buddhism. Temple ties became more a matter of obtaining ritual services for the household dead than a matter of seeking enlightenment.

One stream of religious tradition conspicuous in this period is Shugendō, the way that leads to magico-religious power through ascetic practices in the mountains (see map).[6] A blend of folk Shinto, esoteric Buddhism, and yin-yang Taoist magic,

---

[6] On Shugendō, see Miyake Hitoshi, *Shugendō girei no kenkyū* [Studies in Shugendō ritual], revised and enlarged ed. (Tokyo: Shunjūsha, 1985), *Shugendō shisō no kenkyū* [Studies in Shugendō thought] (Tokyo: Shunjūsha, 1985), *Shugendō jiten* [Shugendō dictionary] (Tokyo: Tōkyōdō Shuppan, 1986) and the 1989 issue of the *Japanese Journal of Religious Studies* devoted to "Shugendo and Mountain Religion in Japan."

this tradition traces its origin to the legend-surrounded shaman En-no-Gyōja of the Nara period (710–794). Several centuries later, under the hereditary Tokugawa shogunate, these once unregulated ascetics were brought under government control as part of an overall policy toward religious movements and organizations.

JAPANESE MOUNTAINS ASSOCIATED WITH MAGICO-RELIGIOUS POWER

During the seventeenth century, Neo-Confucianism came to play an influential role. The Tokugawa shogunate encouraged Confucian studies both in its own schools and in fief schools throughout the nation in order to mold samurai ideas and behavior. In the eighteenth century, through private schools for commoners, Confucian principles spread among craftsmen, merchants and farmers. In the Mito fief (part of what is now Ibaraki Prefecture, located northeast of Tokyo) these studies led to the *Dai Nihon-shi*, a multi-volume history of Japan inculcating the idea of the kami-descended imperial line as the only legitimate basis of authority; it also enlarged the principles of loyalty and filial piety by identifying the emperor as the supreme object of such virtues. These ideas, transmuted during the first half of the nineteenth century into Shinto restorationism, helped bring an end to seven centuries of samurai rule.

SHINTO-BUDDHIST-CHRISTIAN-OTHER PERIOD (1802–)

During the turbulent closing years of the Tokugawa shogunate and the early years of the restoration government, a wave of new religious organizations appeared (see table 2). The harbinger of this development appeared in 1802.

Nyoraikyō, a body classified as Buddhist, began as a faith-healing sect based on the belief that its founder, a peasant woman named Kino (1756–1826), was a living kami and prophet of a better life in the next world. Going against the grain of the highly stratified feudal society of her day, she taught that all people were equal before the Nyorai, whom she identified (contrary to orthodox Buddhist doctrine) as an omniscient, omnipotent creator deity. She further taught that the world was now in its last, degenerate stage, and that all who would devote themselves to this deity could be saved. Kino lived in the Owari fief (much of which is located in what is now Aichi Prefecture) and taught there for a quarter of a century, but the sect she founded was suppressed.[7]

---

[7] After the Meiji Restoration (1868), Nyoraikyō gained a degree of legitimacy by affiliating with the Sōtō school of Zen Buddhism, but with the establishment of State Shinto, it again came under suspicion because of its singular teaching *(cont. on p. 14)*

TABLE 2

ORIGIN AND SIZE OF THE PRINCIPAL NEW RELIGIOUS ORGANIZATIONS

Name	Year of Origin	Members in 1988
	1802–1900	
SHINTO		
Kurozumikyō	1814	295,225
Misogikyō	1840	100,610
Shinrikyō	1843	295,560
Konkōkyō	1859	448,393
Maruyamakyō	1873	9,894
Ontakekyō	1873	622,380
Izumo Ōyashirokyō	1873	1,167,577
Ōmoto	1892	171,821
BUDDHIST		
Nyoraikyō	1802	33,056
Honmon Butsuryūshū	1857	461,296
OTHER		
Tenrikyō	1838	1,777,144
	1901–1945	
SHINTO		
Honmichi	1913	315,673
BUDDHIST		
Kokuchūkai	1914	20,178
Nihonzan Myōhōji Daisanga	1917	1,564
Reiyūkai	1923	3,155,635
Nenpō Shinkyō	1925	807,486
Gedatsukai	1929	238,222
Sōka Gakkai	1930	17,639,866
Kōdō Kyōdan	1935	401,538
Risshō Kōseikai	1938	6,266,750
CHRISTIAN		
Iesu no Mitama Kyōkai Kyōdan	1941	24,090
OTHER		
Ennōkyō	1919	401,789
PL (Perfect Liberty) Kyōdan	1924	2,038,826
Seichō no Ie	1930	817,089
Sekai Kyūseikyō	1934	835,756
	Post-1945	
SHINTO		
Ananaikyō	1949	150,128
BUDDHIST		
Shinnyoen	1948	2,596,102
Myōchikai Kyōdan	1950	917,538
Bussho Gonenkai Kyōdan	1950	2,018,250
Saijō Inarikyō	1951	303,456
OTHER		
Tenshō Kōtai Jingūkyō	1945	454,442
Zenrinkai	1947	594,354

SOURCES: Membership figures, voluntarily reported, represent the situation as of December 31, 1988. The are taken from the 1989 edition of the *Shūkyō nenkan* [Religions yearbook] published in 1990. The list of organizations is adapted from Murakami Shigeyoshi, *Japanese Religion in the Modern Century* (Tokyo: University of Tokyo Press, 1980), 170–71.

Since 1802, three major developments affecting the Japanese people and their institutions have taken place. The first was the "restoration" of the emperor (1868);[8] the second, defeat in war (1945); and the third, economic affluence (from about 1965).

When the restoration government gained control, it disestablished Buddhism and established Shinto in its place. Institutionally intertwined for centuries, Shinto and Buddhism were forcibly separated. The Shugendō organizations, an inseparable amalgam of traditions, were ordered to disband. Many Shugendō ideas and practices, however, were taken up into the "new religions"—ideas such as spirit-possession, exorcism, faith-healing, and attributing to certain religious leaders the status of living kami or living buddhas.[9]

The government classification for the new religions identified as belonging to the Shinto stream was (and is) Sect Shinto.[10] Most Shinto-tradition groups can be understood as belonging to one of four types: Shinto revivalism, purification, sacred mountain, or faith-healing (see table 3).

Among Buddhist groups, Honmon Butsuryūshū, founded in 1857 by the Nichiren priest Nagamatsu Nissen (1817–1890), is significant as the first of the lay Buddhist associations to emphasize conversion to faith in the *Lotus Sūtra* as essential to the welfare of individuals and of the nation.

---

about a creator deity before whom all people were equal. (Under State Shinto such a teaching was equivalent to lèse-majesté.) Subject to persecutions of various kinds for a century and a half, Nyoraikyō became a small, sealed-off institution almost completely closed to outsiders. See Murakami Shigeyoshi, *Shin shūkyō* [New religions] (Tokyo: Hyōronsha, 1980), 15–16, 47–58.

[8] François Macé astutely characterizes the Meiji Restoration as an attempt to combine "an accelerated modernization with a 'restoration' of a mythical imperial rule of pre-Buddhist antiquity. This return to a fictitious past was in fact a mask for a will to break with the past." See "The Funerals of the Japanese Emperors," *Bulletin of the Nanzan Institute for Religion and Culture*, no. 13 (1989), 29.

[9] Capital letters have been employed for "the Buddha" (and the derivatives "Buddhism," "Buddhist," etc.), lowercase letters elsewhere. Thus a Buddhist leader of exceptional character or high office is spoken of as "a living buddha," and the altar for the household dead as the "buddha altar." (Death-related attribution of buddhahood is unique to Japan.)

On "living kami," see Shimazono Susumu, "The Living Kami Idea in the New Religions of Japan," *Japanese Journal of Religious Studies* 6 (1979): 389–412.

[10] The term "Sect Shinto" was originally coined to distinguish new religious organizations from "non-religious" State Shinto.

TABLE 3

TYPES OF NEW RELIGIONS IN THE SHINTO STREAM

Type	Example
Shinto revivalism	Shinrikyō, Izumo Ōyashirokyō
Purification	Misogikyō
Sacred mountain	Maruyamakyō, Ontakekyō
Faith-healing	Kurozumikyō, Tenrikyō, Konkōkyō, Ōmoto

NOTE: Tenrikyō, in order to emphasize its universality, was reclassified as "Other" at its own request in 1970.

From 1859 on, Christian missionaries reintroduced Christianity. Churches, schools and medical care were the main forms through which Christians, Japanese and foreign, sought to plant the new faith. Christianity found a moderate welcome as Japan ended over two centuries of seclusion from the West, but met with disapproval as nationalistic feeling and war fever began to mount from about 1890. It remains a minority religion.

The anti-Buddhist iconoclasm that occurred in many areas with the turn to State Shinto lasted only a few years. When cooler heads prevailed, Buddhism came under government protection and control. Until 1945, however, the mythology of State Shinto increasingly became a rigidly imposed norm. New religious bodies were required to conform or be crushed by state power.[11] The threat was not idle. Particularly after the Religious Organizations Law (*Shūkyō dantai hō*) went into effect in 1940, nonconformist religious bodies, new and old alike, were subjected to severe persecution.[12]

It can be seen that continental Buddhism entered Japan during the shift from clan government to imperial government, a period when a reorientation of values was in process. Buddhism as a popular religion took hold during the shift from imperial to military government, another period of reorientation. Christianity, in turn, arrived during a temporary shift to decentralized

[11] Murakami Shigeyoshi, *Japanese Religion in the Modern Century*, transl. by H. Byron Earhart (Tokyo: University of Tokyo Press, 1980), 48–51, 95–109.
[12] Murakami, *Modern Century*, 74, 97, 103.

domain government, was ousted soon after the restoration of centralized military rule when Neo-Confucian influence was strong, and returned during the swing to a new imperial government under the aegis of Shinto restorationism. The new religious organizations came into being during the decades bracketing the restoration of imperial rule, during the economic depression and totalitarian controls following the First World War, and, to anticipate, during the period of economic and spiritual distress that followed World War II and during the period of economic affluence that began about 1965. In broad perspective, then, it appears that significant religious developments have tended to coincide with periods of political unrest and value-confusion. This finding is reinforced when one considers the religious leaders of these times.

PRE-MODERN RELIGIOUS LEADERS AND THEIR TEACHINGS

One cultural thread evident throughout Japanese history is the tendency to honor only what has a clearly traceable lineage. Arguments supporting the legitimacy of the imperial house rarely fail to mention its "direct and unbroken succession" — a cultural norm even if not a historical fact. In the same way, a person recognized as an outstanding religious leader is frequently revered not only for what he taught but also because he founded a sect that takes pride in tracing its origin back to "the founder."

Saichō (767–822), who studied T'ien-t'ai teachings and disciplines in China, founded the Japanese Tendai sect tradition in 805. He exemplifies a tendency now common among Japanese Buddhists: to seek the absolute not beyond but within the present world. He gave currency to the phrase *sokushin jōbutsu*, "to become a living buddha."[13] This has come to mean that one need not await countless rebirths or undergo endless austerities in order to achieve buddhahood; one can become a living buddha in this lifetime. This teaching has had an immense

---

[13] Nakamura Hajime, *Ways of Thinking of Eastern Peoples: India, China, Tibet, Japan*, rev. English transl., ed. by P. P. Wiener (Honolulu: East-West Center Press, 1964), 363–64.

influence on new Buddhist organizations in the modern period, particularly those that, with Tendai, attach special importance to the *Lotus Sūtra* and its doctrine that all forms of existence, animate and inanimate, are filled with—and can realize—the Buddha nature.

Kūkai (774–835), after studying Tantric Buddhism in China, founded the Japanese Shingon sect in 816. He taught that the entire universe is the body of the Supreme Buddha, Vairocana, and thus that absolute truth and this-worldly phenomena are essentially identical. Synthesizing Buddhist and non-Buddhist philosophies into ten stages of realization culminating in Tantrism, he further taught that meditation, ritual postures, and mystical syllables are uniquely important as symbolic representations of, and channels for, the living substance of the cosmos. This teaching had great influence in the widespread acceptance of ritual practices such as chanting the title of the *Lotus Sūtra*.

Hōnen (1133–1212) and his disciple Shinran (1173–1262) lived at a time when the idea of the impending dissolution of the world was current. Like earlier itinerant holy men, they sought to make the way of enlightenment available to people of all classes and conditions. Both taught that the way of enlightenment most appropriate for "this degenerate age" was not that of ascetic exercises but rather of simple reliance on the power and compassion of Amitābha (in Japanese, Amida) Buddha, who had vowed to help people and was sure to welcome them into his Pure Land.

Hōnen, urging people to call on Amida and gain enlightenment, founded the Pure Land sect in 1175. Shinran, more radical, held that Amida had already fulfilled his vow and that people only needed to accept their enlightenment through faith. This made the celibate monastic life, till then deemed essential to salvation, logically unnecessary. Shinran therefore renounced it, married, and demonstrated that Amida's way applied unconditionally to lay people in the secular world. His organization, the True Pure Land sect, dates from 1224.

The two main forms of Zen Buddhism, Rinzai and Sōtō, were introduced from China by the Japanese priests Eisai (1141–1215) and Dōgen (1200–1253). Eisai, favored by the Kamakura shogunate, taught a way of enlightenment through enigmatic questions called *kōan* that threw the seeker into a quandary but could lead to a flash of saving insight. His ties were mainly with the newly dominant samurai class. Dōgen, more reliant on scriptural authority than on political patronage, taught that the way to enlightenment is through *shikan taza,* "seated meditation alone." His ties were mainly with the unlettered and often superstitious peasant class.

Nichiren (1222–1282) is by far the most confrontational of Japanese religious leaders, and the sect tradition that bears his name has been the most prone to schism. Like many before him, including Saichō and Dōgen, Nichiren treated the *Lotus Sūtra* as the highest scriptural authority, but unlike his predecessors, he taught that it was imperative for the welfare of Japan that the government rid the nation of false ways (primarily the Shingon, Zen, and Pure Land sects) and establish as the state religion the true Buddhism he proclaimed. This teaching, in subsequent variations, looms large in the development of several new religious organizations.

In the Shinto world Yoshida Kanetomo (1435–1511), founder of Yoshida Shinto, took as his point of departure a thirteenth-century school of thought called Ise Shinto. In contrast to Buddhist thinkers who had interpreted the Shinto kami as demigods in need of enlightenment or, later, as avataras of specific buddhas and bodhisattvas, Ise Shinto took the position that the basic reality of the universe was a kami through whom the buddhas and bodhisattvas had their being. Yoshida, going a step further, sought to develop a Shinto free of Buddhist influences by emphasizing purity of heart as a mystical form of worship.

Japanese Neo-Confucianism began with Fujiwara Seika (1561–1619). Both he and his illustrious disciple, Hayashi Razan (1583–1657), one of the most influential Confucian advisors to the first Tokugawa shogun, taught that the way of Confucius was virtuous in so far as it fitted into the way of the kami, the way of the emperor. They regarded Buddhism as inferior for teaching a universal law that concealed differential obligations according to social rank. As often noted, the traditional Confucian doctrines of abdication and justifiable rebellion could not be accommodated in Japan. Under Tokugawa Mitsukuni (1628–1700), founder of the Mito school, Neo-Confucian teachings were recast in such a way as to uphold the superiority of the emperor over daimyo and shogun, yet also in such a way as to soften the distinction between ruler and ruled by presenting the emperor as a caring father.

Motoori Norinaga (1730–1801), a renowned scholar and interpreter of classical Japanese literature, became the founder of a movement to purify Shinto of all Buddhist and Confucian accretions. His self-proclaimed disciple Hirata Atsutane (1776–1843) went even further, developing into an anti-foreign chauvinist as he promoted restoration of power to the imperial house.

The ninth century, when Saichō and Kūkai introduced new forms of continental Buddhism, marks the conclusion of a wave of cultural influx from China.[14] The twelfth and thirteenth centuries, when Hōnen, Shinran, Eisai, Dōgen, and Nichiren began to spread Buddhism among the common people, mark the period when political power shifted from the imperial court in Kyoto to the military government in Kamakura. The period from 1477 to 1573, during which Yoshida Shinto was born, is known in Japan as the *sengoku jidai,* the period of warring states. The Shinto-informed Neo-Confucianism that took shape at the hand of Fujiwara Seika and his successors came into being when an alarmed shogunate was establishing measures to eliminate Christianity. Hirata Atsutane's idea of imperial supremacy as the heart of a purified Shinto appeared in the first half of the nineteenth century, a period when international challenges to Japan's isolation were intensifying. Again it appears, therefore, that significant religious developments have tended to coincide with periods of social and political unrest.

---

[14] Sugimoto Masayoshi and David L. Swain, *Science and Culture in Traditional Japan: A.D. 600–1854* (Cambridge, Massachusetts: MIT Press, 1978; Rutland, Vermont and Tokyo, Japan: Charles E. Tuttle Co., 1989), xxv, 10, 40–42.

RELIGION IN CONTEMPORARY JAPAN

A STATISTICAL PICTURE

The estimated population of Japan on October 1, 1988 was nearly 123 million. Of this number, how many people belonged to religious organizations? More broadly, how many regarded themselves as religious?

To answer the first question, data from the *Shūkyō nenkan* [Religions yearbook] are usually employed. But immediately one confronts an anomaly. In 1988 the total number of adherents claimed for the major classes of religious tradition was 191 million, a figure about 55 percent larger than the total population of Japan (see graph 2, based on the figures in table 1). This "discrepancy" is generally accounted for by two facts: dual or multiple affiliation, and inflated membership reports. Whatever the case, it is useless to compare population figures with membership figures in the hope of determining what proportion of the population belongs to religious organizations and what proportion does not. One can, however, consider survey findings. One survey, published in 1979, asked people about their membership in organizations of various kinds. With regard to religious organizations, only 13.6 percent said they were members.[15] This percentage, applied to the 1988 population, suggests that only 16.7 million out of 123 million people counted themselves as adherents of religious organizations.

Living religion is by no means limited to members of religious organizations. Another survey conducted in 1979 asked people if they professed any religious faith. Affirmative replies to this question amounted to 33.6 percent.[16] Most people replying in the affirmative went on to identify their faith as Buddhist (78.4%). Only a handful (3.3%) identified their faith as Shinto — almost certainly Sect Shinto rather than the district-organized Shrine Shinto in which the question of faith rarely occurs. But

---

[15] Fujii Masao, "Gendaijin no shūkyō kōdō" [The religious behavior of contemporary Japanese people], *Jurisuto*, no. 21 (1981), 133.

[16] Fujii, "Shūkyō kōdō" [Religious behavior], 133.

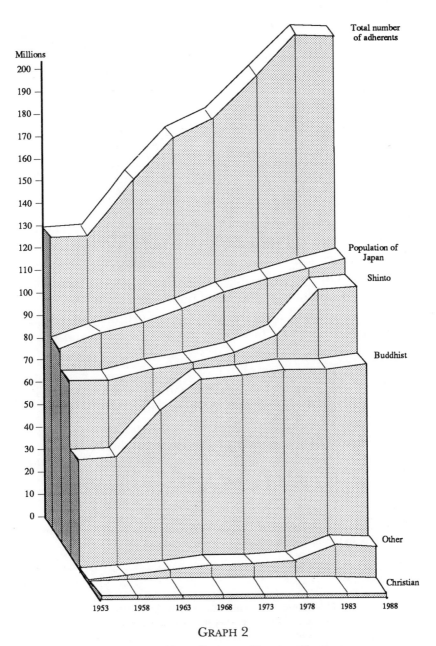

GRAPH 2

ADHERENTS TO MAJOR CLASSES OF RELIGIOUS TRADITION

since most Japanese people of religious persuasion are both Shinto parishioners and Buddhist temple supporters, it is perhaps not unreasonable to suppose that about the same number of people can be found in both camps. If so, the religious population of present-day Japan can be reckoned at about one-third of the total population.[17]

RELIGIOUS PRACTICES

Before 1945 the ideal-type Japanese household traditionally had both a kami altar (*kamidana*) and a buddha altar (*butsudan*). To a lesser extent, the same holds true today. Rural households, especially, often have several kami altars: one main altar and other minor altars. In a rough division of labor, the kami altar is generally associated with life and the avoidance of whatever impedes vitality and productivity, the buddha altar with death and the veneration of those who are becoming or have become ancestors.[18] On both, offerings of food and drink are presented at the beginning of each day. (See photos in chapter 6.)

The Shinto and Buddhist practices of ordinary people may be grouped under two headings: the annual cycle and the life cycle. (For a list of major festivals see table 4; for a picture of the pattern they form see graph 3.)

The New Year season involves a number of activities now largely associated with Shinto. Some of these activities are oriented to the household, some to the national community.

At the end of a year, households throughout the land "clean the slate" by giving the house, yard, and adjacent road a thorough cleaning and by paying off all debts due. Entrances are

---

[17] Nishiyama notes that, according to a survey conducted every five years since 1958 by the Tōkei Sūri Kenkyūsho, the percentage of people who affirm personal religious faith diminished for a number of years, hitting a low of 25 percent in 1973, but in 1978 jumping back up to 34.5 percent. See Ōmura Eishō and Nishiyama Shigeru, eds., *Gendaijin no shūkyō* [The religion of present-day people] (Tokyo: Yūhikaku, 1988), 192.

[18] During the years that rituals are performed for the deceased individual, he or she is in process of becoming an ancestor. After performance of the concluding ritual (*tomuraiage*), usually thirty-three years after death, the deceased is regarded not as an individual but as one with "the body of ancestors." (For a more detailed account, see chapter 5, "Remembering the Dead.")

decorated with evergreens and shafts of cut bamboo. (According to the widely accepted theory of Yanagita Kunio, New Year was originally a festival to welcome the ancestral spirits, apparently conceived of as diminutive, like songbirds or fireflies. He regarded the bamboo shafts as their "landing sites.") For three days or so, people lay aside their daily work in order to be with their families, send out New Year's greetings, call on and give gifts to elderly relatives, teachers and others. They wear their best clothes and eat special foods. Today, any awareness of the purported connection between New Year and the ancestors is dim, except that if a family loses one of its members, it will not celebrate the next New Year.

TABLE 4

ANNUAL CYCLE OF MAJOR FESTIVALS

Date or period	Japanese name	English paraphrase
January 1–6	*shōgatsu*	New Year
February 3	*setsubun*	Turn of the seasons
March 3	*hina matsuri*	Doll festival
March 21	*haru no higan*	Vernal equinox
April 8	*hana matsuri*	Flower festival [Buddha's birthday]
April–May	*taue matsuri*	Rice-planting festivals †
June 15	*suijin matsuri*	Water kami festival
June 30	*ōharai*	Grand purification
* July 13-16	*bon*	Feast of lights
* August 15	*tsukimi*	Moonviewing
* August	*kaza matsuri*	Wind festivals †
September 23	*aki no higan*	Autumnal equinox
October–November	*shūkaku matsuri*	Harvest festivals †
December 1	*suijin matsuri*	Water kami festival
December 31	*ōharai*	Grand purification

NOTE: For explanations of these and other festivals, see Hori et al., *Japanese Religion*, 126–32; for a remarkable essay on one local festival, see Yanagawa Keiichi, "Theological and Scientific Thinking about Festivals," *Japanese Journal of Religious Studies* 1 (1974): 5–49.

* These dates and periods are those of the traditional lunisolar calendar, presently about one month ahead of the Western calendar used in Japan since 1873.

† Where the word "festivals" occurs, festival dates vary with the locality.

Closer to the spirit of national community is the practice of visiting a big-name shrine or temple at the beginning of a new year. According to police estimates, the number of people who visited such institutions rose from 25 million (roughly 25% of the population) in 1965 to 80 million (nearly 65% of the population) in 1990.

The midsummer feast of lights, or Bon festival, is a community activity in which, traditionally, individual households welcome their visiting ancestral spirits and entertain them communally. At this time the house is thoroughly cleaned, then

GRAPH 3

PATTERN OF MAJOR ANNUAL FESTIVALS

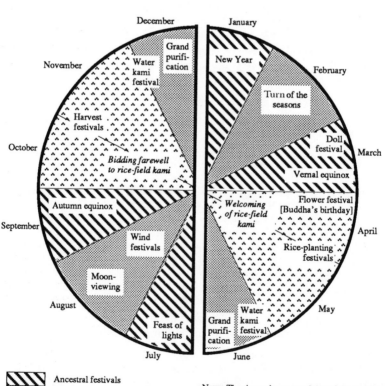

Ancestral festivals

Festivals of exorcism and purification

Agricultural festivals

NOTE: The times shown are those of the traditional lunisolar calendar, presently about one month ahead of the Western calendar used in Japan since 1873.

decorated with fresh fruit and flowers. Meat foods are generally taboo. A small welcoming fire is built just outside the gate in order to guide the spirits. People dress up in light, summer-weight kimonos, and entire communities hold outdoor dances and displays of fireworks to celebrate the occasion. The Bon festival closes with "seeing-off" fires, usually made of twigs and again located just outside the household gate. In some areas people prepare hundreds of tiny floats, often bearing a lighted candle, and at nightfall set them adrift on streams or lakes. (Not all such floats spring from this motive, however. Some are simply to create a pleasant scene and to attract tourists.) Most of today's urban residents or their recent forebears came from a rural area where the "old homestead" is still located and where the ancestral tablets are kept—though this state of affairs is rapidly changing. Millions of people, therefore, still travel to the country for the Bon festival family reunions and return to the cities a few days later.[19] Officially, the Bon festival is not a national holiday. Some idea of its importance to ordinary people can be gained, however, from the realization that over half the industries in Japan give workers a few days off at this time.

The spring and autumn equinoxes are also times when the ancestors are honored. Trips to the "old homestead" are not necessary. Instead, a few relatives get together and visit the family grave in their area. They clean and sweep the site, pour water on the gravestone, present flowers and incense and perhaps food and drink, and offer silent prayer. If nobody has died

---

[19] This link between urban and rural areas has weakened in recent years because of the postwar establishment of legally independent nuclear families. This has led not only to the consequent need for new family graves, but also to a shift in perspective regarding the spirits of the family dead. Formerly they were regarded as powerful protectors. Today the tendency is to regard them with affection as beings whose welfare in the next world depends on the ritual observances of living kin. (Some new religions teach that people who experience declining fortunes, sickness, or the threat of death are being punished by a neglected ancestral spirit. This teaching is particularly evident in Reiyūkai and groups that have split away from it.) On this matter as a whole, see Kōmoto Mitsugu, "Gendai toshi no minzoku shinkō: Kakyō saiken to chinkon" [Folk religion in the modern city: Relocating the family home and the repose of souls]. In Ōmura and Nishiyama, eds., *Gendaijin* [Present-day people], 33–75. On Reiyūkai, see Helen Hardacre, *Lay Buddhism in Contemporary Japan: Reiyūkai Kyōdan* (Princeton: Princeton University Press, 1984).

recently and the pain of parting has passed, the occasion may well be a happy one, with the children playing games and all enjoying a picnic.

Community-wide festivals associated with Shinto shrines are usually held once or twice a year. The timing varies with the community, but the major festivals follow much the same pattern: a formal service for purification of the parish representatives and for invocation of the kami; removal of the kami-symbol from the inner sanctuary and its ritual installation in a scaled-down portable shrine (often weighing several tons); a solemn or boisterous procession whereby the kami tours and infuses new life into the parish; a feast at the shrine where the priest and parish representatives enjoy food, drink and entertainment expressive of the new vigor bestowed by the kami; and the formal (and sometimes secret) rite of ushering the kami back into the inner sanctuary.[20] In small, rural communities, as young people leave for the towns and cities, it becomes increasingly difficult to hold festivals in the usual way. Not uncommonly, the scaled-down shrine now has to be borne not on the shoulders of stalwart young men chanting in rhythm but on a truck equipped with a loudspeaker. Conversely, in growing communities festivals find considerable support, usually for a combination of reasons, sometimes mainly religious, at other times mainly secular.

The life cycle has its focus in the individual, but its context is the family. Birth is associated with the local Shinto shrine. On or about the thirtieth day after birth, the child is taken to the shrine and presented to the kami. From that time on, the child is under the care of the divinity. This point receives ritual reinforcement a few years later when girls of three and seven years of age, and boys of five, are dressed up and taken to the shrine in mid-November for a brief ceremony.

Marriage did not become a religious ritual until the twentieth century. Since 1901, when the first Shinto wedding was performed, Shinto rites have gradually become the accepted way of uniting households through matrimony, though Christian

---

[20] For an excellent analysis of the festival process, see Sonoda Minoru, "The Traditional Festival in Urban Society," *Japanese Journal of Religious Studies* 2 (1975): 103–36.

rites (not necessarily requiring faith) are becoming increasingly popular.

Death is by far the most complex rite of passage. Buddhism is the main religious tradition involved, but the postwar legal abolition of the extended family and its replacement by the nuclear family is leading to a different way of identifying the ancestors. Until 1945 the ancestors in the paternal line were the principal objects of veneration. Women who married out of the family had their names struck out of the family record, and affines were treated, in death, more as guests than as family members. Since 1945, however, many people, especially those in their thirties and forties, are coming to venerate both the paternal and maternal lines. As before, the process of becoming an ancestor calls for thirty-three to fifty years of ritual observances, some at the Buddhist temple, others before the buddha altar in the home.

POST–1945 DEVELOPMENTS

NEW RELIGIONS IN THE MODERNIZATION STREAM

After 1945, as a direct result of defeat in war, religious freedom supported by government neutrality vis-à-vis religion became a constitutional principle for the first time in Japanese history. In this new situation hundreds of new religious organizations sprang up. Most proved ephemeral, some downright fraudulent. Most of the sizable groups trace their origin to the years between the first and second world wars, but it was after 1945 that they grew by leaps and bounds (see table 5). This growth provided part of the stimulus for internal reform movements among several older bodies.

With regard to new religious organizations that became prominent during the period 1945–1970, those to be mentioned may be considered representative of many.[21] The most conspicuous organizations, like Honmon Butsuryūshū before them, are

---

[21] See Hori, *Japanese Religion*, 89–104.

associations of lay Buddhists who honor the *Lotus Sūtra* and seek to reform Japanese society.

TABLE 5

GROWTH INDEXES FOR MAJOR CLASSES OF RELIGIOUS TRADITION

YEAR	RELIGIOUS TRADITION			
	Shinto	Buddhism	Christianity	Other
1953	100.0	100.0	100.0	100.0
1958	98.8	102.6	134.4	117.3
1963	103.2	146.4	146.6	156.5
1968	107.3	174.5	171.3	197.9
1973	112.4	177.2	181.2	292.5
1978	126.7	184.5	195.8	401.5
1983	150.3	183.3	324.4	434.3
1988	143.7	195.1	293.1	332.7

NOTE: For each classification, the number of adherents reported for 1953 (see table 1) is assigned a value of 100.

Two currents may be distinguished. The first is the Sōka Gakkai current. Largest of all the new religions, Sōka Gakkai is theoretically under the Nichiren Shōshū, a monastic organization that claims exclusive legitimacy as heir to the teachings of Nichiren. One of the fundamental goals of the Nichiren Shōshū is to see the emperor and the government converted to the form of Buddhism it proclaims as exclusively true. Religious freedom and government neutrality toward religion have no place in its world view. But its independently formed lay association, Sōka Gakkai, has come out in favor of religious freedom and separation of state and religion. The short history of the relationship between Sōka Gakkai and the Nichiren Shōshū, not to mention the latter's other lay associations, has been one of tension and near-schism. Through its network of neighborhood groups, however, Sōka Gakkai has brought help to millions of people more concerned about personal problems than about abstract questions of principle and authority.

The second stream runs through the tradition connecting Reiyūkai and one of its many offshoots, Risshō Kōseikai. The importance of memorial rites for ancestors and faith in the *Lotus Sūtra* are the two main tenets of Reiyūkai.[22] Particularly notable in this group is its practice of having members venerate ancestors in both the paternal and maternal lines. Some scholars derive this practice from the circumstance that in its early days Reiyūkai drew its members from economically peripheral families in which both parents had to work for pay. At any rate, it anticipated the bilateral memorial rites increasingly practiced among Japanese families in general since legal entitlement of the nuclear family and at least token acceptance of the idea of male-female equality.

Risshō Kōseikai likewise honors the *Lotus Sūtra* and the ancestors, but its distinctive emphasis has been on perfection of the individual through group counselling circles where leaders give guidance on personal problems in the light of sutra teaching. Unlike Sōka Gakkai, which has direct connections with the political world through its formally autonomous party (the Kōmeitō), Risshō Kōseikai, in company with other new religious organizations, has chosen not to form a political party but to form friendships with political figures and, as occasion demands, to exercise influence indirectly through dialogue and through the votes of its members. Its social-reform concerns may be seen in the work of its interreligious agency, the World Conference on Religion and Peace.

The principal reason that people join new religious organizations of this type is to find help with health, marital, financial, and other problems. The nature of the help offered varies. In general, however, one can perceive a tendency to affirm that health, wealth, and happiness can be obtained if a person will only have implicit faith in the leader and in the divinity or divine reality he or she represents, share the story of how "conversion" has changed life for the better,[23] participate wholeheartedly in the activities of the organization, and win new members by holding out the promise of the help available through this

[22] Cf. Hardacre, *Reiyūkai.*

[23] See Shimazono Susumu, "Conversion Stories and their Popularization in Japan's New Religions," *Japanese Journal of Religious Studies* 13 (1986): 157–75.

supportive fellowship. Because they often blended doctrinal interpretations with elements of folk religion and even magical practices, the new religious organizations were at first viewed with suspicion and disdain by educated people. In recent years, however, many of the new bodies have to some extent rid themselves of such features, rationalized their operations, and reached a stage where leaders are no longer likely to be regarded as near divine wonderworkers. New religious organizations that came to prominence between 1945 and 1970 now represent principles that tend, on the whole, to support the rational, anti-magical aims of modernization.

NEW RELIGIONS OF MAGIC AND MIRACLE

Since about 1970, a further class of new religions has attracted the attention of many students of Japanese religion and society. With names like GLA, Agonshū, Byakkō Shinkōkai, Mahikari and the like, names that sound exotic even in Japanese, organizations of this type, even if founded before 1970, have drawn many members during the past two decades.[24] By and large they tend to attribute primary importance to messages from the spirit world communicated by *reinōsha* or mediums who sometimes speak in tongues, to rely on faith-healing by means of spiritual waves said to emanate from a healer's palm, to employ esoteric or exorcistic rituals intended to pacify angry ancestral spirits allegedly identified as the cause of present suffering both in the individual and in the larger society, and to claim that all these elements from the particularistic world of Japanese folk religion serve the universal cause of world peace.

---

[24] In round figures GLA (the God Light Association) currently has over 12,000 members (in addition to which there are many groups that have split off from it for which few statistics are available: Kokoro no Tsudoi, Ashram Tokyo, Ishiki Kyōiku Kenkyūsho, Ai no Family Kyōkai, Kokusai Shōhō Kyōkai, Kaiwakai, Kōfuku no Kagaku, and Hikari no Onakama); Agonshū has over 200,000, Byakkō Shinkōkai 500,000, and the Mahikari organizations (Sekai Mahikari Bunmei Kyōdan and its offshoots: Sūkyō Mahikari, Shinyūgen Kyūsei Mahikari Bunmei Kyōdan and Subikari Kōha Sekai Shindan) a combined total of over 500,000. See the *Shūkyō nenkan* (1990), 128–31 and the *Shinshūkyō jiten* (1990), 88–90, 129, 708, 712, 727, 728, and 736. For a thoughtful analysis of Agonshū, see Ian Reader, "The Rise of a Japanese 'New New Religion': Themes in the Development of Agonshū," *Japanese Journal of Religious Studies* 15 (1988): 235–61.

Why religions oriented to spiritualist magic should make their appearance at this time is a moot point, but at least three interrelated factors seem to be involved: (1) there is general agreement that an unusually high percentage of the adherents to these religions are in their twenties and thirties,[25] (2) people of this age group would have received their public school education under the new Constitution, which forbids religion in the curriculum, and (3) organizations of the type under discussion include some that are explicitly religious (for example, Agonshū, a body legally incorporated as a religious organization) and some that avoid the name religion (as in Kōfuku no Kagaku, "the science of happiness"). Taken together, these factors suggest that there may be some connection between the search for meaning in the midst of affluence, the separation of religious principles from public education, and the existence of organizations that offer meaning and supportive fellowship under the name of religion or a quasi-religious substitute. In any case it is certain that the new religious organizations that came to prominence between 1970 and 1990 represent principles that tend, on the whole, to run counter to the rational, anti-magical aims of modernization.

The affluence following the high growth rates that began about 1965 signifies a change unprecedented in Japanese social history.[26] Earlier it was seen that new religious developments accompany significant sociopolitical change. Now it appears that new religious developments also accompany significant socioeconomic change. This is not to say that social change *causes* new religious organizations to arise. Nor is it to say that social change

---

[25] Cf. Ōmura and Nishiyama, eds., *Gendaijin* [Present-day people], 202. It is also worth noting that in 1965 the total number of university and junior college students in Japan exceeded 1 million for the first time (28% in government schools, 72% in private.

[26] In December 1960 the Cabinet decided on a high growth rate economic policy. The effects became evident between 1965 and 1973, when double-digit growth rates were the rule. The next decade showed more moderate figures. (In 1966 the growth rate was 10.8%, in 1968 14.2%, in 1969 12.1%, in 1970 10.3%, in 1971 5.2%, in 1972 9.5%, and in 1973 10.0%. In 1976 the growth rate was 5.3%, in 1977 5.3%, in 1978 5.1%, in 1979 5.2%, in 1980 4.8%, in 1981 4.1%, in 1982 3.3%, and in 1983 3.0%.) Figures taken from the *Nihon shūkyō jiten* [Dictionary of Japanese religions] (1985), 923–46.

can explain their continuing existence. But it has been shown, I believe, that social change and religious development are interwoven—even where religious development is no longer recognized as religious.

Living religion in Japan involves more than annual and life-cycle rites of passage, internal reform in established organizations, and new religious organizations that promise help with personal problems. It also involves questions of law and state power. For over a thousand years, government officials and religious leaders alike took it for granted that government could legitimately police religious organizations in the interests of the state. The year 1945 brought changes that led to constitutional and legal institutionalization of the value of government neutrality toward religious organizations. This value is less than fifty years old in Japanese institutional history. Its meaning is a subject of public debate, legal action, and political maneuver. In what changing forms religious freedom will survive in a Japan that values both tradition and internationalism remains to be seen.

Chapter 2

Religion and State in Japan, 1965–1990

T
HE QUESTION OF HOW to interpret current changes in
Japanese religion and society leads to much headshaking.
Its difficulty is made even more complicated by the fact
that interpretations differ depending on whether the interpreter
presupposes one or the other of the two forms of religious
existence that predominate in present-day Japan. Both forms
rest on the assumption that religious phenomena have to do with
the human relation to the sacred, however conceived. Despite
this common assumption, the two forms of religious existence
are fundamentally different. The suggestion to be made here is
not that these two forms, singly or together, are "uniquely
Japanese," but that their relationship includes a political dimension that must be taken into account when we seek to understand
recent changes in Japanese religion and society.[1]

Yanagawa and Abe, in a thought-provoking article with the
outrageous title "Cross-cultural Implications of a Behavioral
Response," speak of these two forms of religious existence as
community religiosity and individual religiosity.[2]

---

[1] For a thought-provoking collection of essays on recent changes in Japanese religion and society, see Yanagawa Keiichi, ed., *Gendai shakai to shūkyō* [Modern society
and religion] (Tokyo: Tōyō Tetsugaku Kenkyūsho, 1978).

[2] Yanagawa Keiichi and Abe Yoshiya, *Japanese Journal of Religious Studies* 10
(1983): 289–307.

"Community religiosity" has to do with the organization and mobilization of people and resources in a natural community for ritual behavior that involves community members as representatives of groups. A monument commemorating local soldiers who lost their lives in military service, for example, is often the site of a natural community ritual. At such a ritual, participation by representation is the rule. A household head is expected to attend, but may, if unavoidably occupied, send his wife to take his place. Local government officials are expected to participate by virtue of their office. The ritual itself is likely to be either Shinto or Buddhist in form, but the priest is more of an invited guest than a principal. In community religiosity the question of personal faith does not arise. In fact it is widely accepted that in a matter of this kind, one demonstrates civic responsibility by putting the community first, whatever one's personal faith. Participation signifies reliability. It is a way of showing, and confirming, one's identity as a member of the community.

"Individual religiosity" as generally understood in Japan today has to do with personal adherence to particular beliefs, religious organizations, or faith-communities. Joining a new religion, for example, or becoming a member of a Christian church, are instances of individual religiosity. In this case the idea of participation by representation has no place. One cannot send a spouse as a substitute. Government officials are welcome, but in principle at least, no weight attaches to their office. Within the religious organization, the priest or other specialist, however named, has a central and leading role. Not all religious organizations emphasize personal faith in a deity or transcendent reality, but there is a general tendency to emphasize loyalty and gratitude to living leaders, especially those who help with personal or domestic problems, sometimes at great personal sacrifice.

In Japanese tradition generally, community religiosity has priority over individual religiosity. If we imagine two concentric circles, community religiosity would be the larger circle, individual religiosity the smaller. The natural community embraces particular faith-communities. Individual religiosity is subordinate to community religiosity.

This description of community religiosity and individual religiosity and of the relationship between the two might serve as an ideal-type model for Japanese religion from about 1868 to 1888, the first two decades of the Meiji period (1868–1912). In addition it may perhaps serve as an indication of the direction in which recent court cases concerning religion seem to be headed. But between the model for the past and the model for the future stand developments of considerable complexity. Taking the Yanagawa-Abe article as my point of departure, I propose to review the main developments and see what they portend for religious freedom in Japan.

THE *SAISEI ITCHI* TRADITION

When the Tokugawa shogunate decided, after 1854, to end its two centuries of seclusion and establish diplomatic relationships with other nations, it tottered and in the final days of 1867 gave way to a new form of government committed to modernization under an allegedly "restored" imperial rule.[3] In the spring of 1868 the new government established its basic policy with regard to religion: *saisei itchi*, "the unity of religion and government."

Saisei itchi has never meant "theocracy" in the sense of a professional priesthood ruling in the name of a god or gods. It has meant that the emperor was revered as a descendant of "the Deity who established the State" and that religious organizations have been considered, and have usually considered themselves, as rightly at the service of the state.[4]

Guided by the policy of the unity of religion and state, the government revived an ancient name, the *Jingikan*, or "Department of Shinto Affairs," gave this department authority over Shinto shrines throughout the nation, and disestablished Buddhism.[5] Christianity remained a forbidden religion, and in a

---

[3] See chap. 1, n. 8.

[4] Anesaki Masaharu, *History of Japanese Religion* (Rutland, Vermont and Tokyo, Japan: Charles E. Tuttle, 1963), 20.

[5] Bereft of government recognition, Buddhism had no legal right to exist and was exposed to anti-Buddhist iconoclasm until 1877, when the government established

continuation of shogunate practice, public notices warning against Christianity were erected early in 1868.

Impressed and disturbed by the military power of Western governments, and provoked by unequal treaty provisions imposed by foreign powers, the Meiji government in 1871 sent the Iwakura Mission to visit Western countries in order to take soundings and advise on future policy. Everywhere it went, the Iwakura Mission encountered, as it seems to have expected, severe criticism because of Japan's prohibition against Christianity.[6] The Mission advised, therefore, that the government give legal recognition to the Christian religion. Public notices proscribing Christianity were removed in 1873, and an article on religious freedom was included in the Meiji Constitution of 1890.[7] At this point it seemed that individual religiosity had the advantage.

The year 1890, however, also saw the issuing of the Imperial Rescript on Education. In strongly Confucian terms, this rescript held up the values of loyalty to the emperor and harmony in social relations, thus affirming the responsibility of subordinates toward superiors. By implication, it laid out for the new age the basic principles of social organization and morals, principles later made the basis of moral instruction in government schools throughout the nation. The Imperial Rescript on Education served, then, as a counterpoise to the Constitution.[8] It showed that community religiosity was still the dominant tradition and

---

the *Shaji Kyoku*, or "Bureau of Shinto Shrines and Buddhist Temples," in the Ministry of Home Affairs.

[6] Abe Yoshiya, "From Prohibition to Toleration: Japanese Government Views Regarding Christianity, 1854–73," *Japanese Journal of Religious Studies* 5 (1978): 107–38.

According to Calvin Parker, the Baptist missionary Jonathan Goble was one of the first to communicate with members of the Iwakura Mission, since he met them on board the U.S.S. *America* as they were en route to the U.S. It seems that they had already decided to recommend lifting the ban on Christianity, but were seeking "foreign pressure" to counter xenophobic resistance at home. Cf. F. Calvin Parker, *Jonathan Goble of Japan: Marine, Missionary, Maverick* (Lanham, Maryland: University Press of America, 1990), 179–82.

[7] The exact name is the *Dai Nippon Teikoku Kenpō* (Imperial constitution of the great empire of Japan), commonly referred to as the Meiji Constitution. It was promulgated on February 11, 1889 and went into effect on November 29, 1890.

[8] Yanagawa and Abe, "Cross-cultural Implications," 294–95.

that individual religiosity would be tolerated only insofar as it did not interfere.

Logically, however, a semantic problem remained. It was generally recognized that in contrast to Christianity, which emphasized doctrine, individual belief, and the community of faith, Shinto was more oriented to ritual on behalf of the natural community, whether expressed in the kinship unit, the village, or the nation.[9] To allow equal rights to these two forms of religious existence was out of the question. Yet as long as Shinto and Christianity alike were labeled "religion," the constitutional guarantee of religious freedom seemed to apply equally to both. How to preserve the constitutional guarantee and still make it clear that community religiosity took priority over individual religiosity was the problem.

The solution was simple: to identify Shinto as a nonreligious moral obligation binding on all imperial subjects, whatever their personal religion. Buddhism was a religion, Christianity was a religion, even Sect Shinto belonged to the category of religion, but Shrine Shinto was not a religion.

In 1900 this way of resolving the problem was institutionalized by establishing two separate agencies in the Ministry of Home Affairs: a *Jinja Kyoku*, or "Shrine Bureau," and a *Shūkyō Kyoku*, or "Religions Bureau." In 1913 the distinction was made even more emphatic by transferring the Religions Bureau to the Ministry of Education.[10] Thus "religion" was administratively defined to mean individual religiosity. Community religiosity, though obligatory for all, was for administrative purposes no longer a religion.

The law that codified these developments in the *saisei itchi* tradition was the Religious Organizations Law (*Shūkyō dantai hō*). Promulgated in April 1939 and legally binding from January 1, 1940, the Religious Organizations Law provided an avenue by which religious bodies could apply for and receive, subject to

---

[9] Where the word "Shinto" stands without a qualifying adjective, the reference is not to *kyōha shintō* ("Sect Shinto") but to *jinja shintō* ("Shrine Shinto").

[10] "In 1940 even the parallelism of titles was eliminated when the Shrine Bureau was renamed the Department of Shrine Affairs (*jingi-in*)." Kawawata, "Religious Organizations," 163.

government authorization, legal recognition as private juridical persons. The organizations eventually recognized under this law were thirteen Sect Shinto groups, twenty-eight Buddhist sects, and two Christian churches: the Roman Catholic Church and the United Church of Christ in Japan (originally a federation of thirty-four Protestant denominations and sects).[11]

Kawawata offers a balanced assessment of the Religious Organizations Law:

> On the positive side, the Religious Organizations Law, by enabling religious bodies to become incorporated as private juridical persons, presented authorized groups with certain advantages. Not only did they then occupy a clearly defined position within the legal structure, they were also in a stronger position as regards corporate ownership and disposition of property. Moreover, under this law Christian organizations were for the first time given a legal status equal to that of Buddhist and Sect Shinto organizations. On the other hand, this law also put into the hands of the state a battery of regulations to supervise and control the organizations it authorized. In applying the law, government authorities did not hesitate to interfere in the internal affairs of these organizations. As a result the Religious Organizations Law became an instrument for obstructing religious freedom.[12]

Between 1868 and 1945, then, the *saisei itchi* tradition provided the value-orientation by which the state defined the terms

---

[11] Shrine Shinto organizations came under a different legal authority (Ministry of Home Affairs Ordinance No. 2 of 1913) and were classified as public juridical persons. Because of the special nature of its connection with the state, the Shrine Shinto of this period is commonly spoken of as State Shinto.

[12] Kawawata, "Religious Organizations," 163–64. William P. Woodard, *The Allied Occupation of Japan 1945–1952 and Japanese Religions* (Leiden: E. J. Brill, 1972), 50–51, n. 1, if more negative, is more specific: "The more objectionable provisions of the Religious Organizations Law . . . were: (1) a religious organization had to secure the approval of the competent minister or its prefectural governor before (a) it could come into existence (Arts. III and VI), (b) its chosen head could assume office (Art. IV–4); (c) its regulations could be changed (Arts. III–2, VI–3); and (d) it could be dissolved (Art. V – XI–2); and (2) the competent minister had the power 'to limit, prohibit, or suspend' the activities of a religious body if it did anything regarded as 'disturbing to peace and order or counter to the duties of Subjects' or 'injurious to public welfare' (Arts. XVI, XVII, XXXVI)."

on which religious organizations would be allowed to exist. Religious freedom, though guaranteed by the Meiji Constitution, applied only to voluntary individual religiosity. Community religiosity, carefully defined as nonreligious, was obligatory for all.

THE *SEIKYŌ BUNRI* TRADITION

In 1945 a different tradition was inaugurated: the tradition of *seikyō bunri*, or "separation of religion and state." This tradition was not without Japanese advocates even prior to 1945, notably among liberal intellectuals, Christians, and Communists. But its institutionalization in Japanese law began under the Occupation (1945–1952).[13]

The Constitution of Japan was promulgated on November 3, 1946 and went into effect on May 3, 1947.[14] Two articles have particular reference to religion and the state. Article 20 guarantees freedom of religion and the separation of religion and state. Article 89 forbids the use of public funds for religious purposes.[15]

---

[13] Occupation directives such as the "Abolition of Governmental Sponsorship, Support, Perpetuation, Control, and Dissemination of State Shinto (*Kokka Shinto, Jinja Shinto*)" of December 15, 1945, commonly known as the Shinto Directive, initiated the policy of separation of religion and state well before the new Constitution went into effect. The basis for codifying this policy in Japanese law, however, is the new Constitution.

[14] Abe Yoshiya—in Tamaru Noriyoshi, ed., *Gendai tennō to shintō* [The emperor and Shinto today] (Tokyo: Tokuma Shoten, 1990), 63–5—points out that GHQ first requested the Japanese government to come up with a draft, and that it did so. But the draft produced was merely a slightly altered version of the Meiji Constitution. Because of the changing international situation and the strong possibility that the U.S.S.R. would seek to influence the shaping of the new constitution, a possibility the U.S. wanted to avoid, it was decided that the GHQ Government Section should produce the first draft.

Abe is careful to explain, however, that the new Constitution was not imposed on the Japanese government by GHQ. It was proposed for consideration. The Japanese side received GHQ arguments in favor of the various provisions, made their own evaluation, and prepared the new Constitution in accordance with the amendment procedures spelled out in the Meiji Constitution.

[15] Article 20, Section 3 reads: "The State and its organs shall refrain from religious education or any other religious activity."

Article 89 reads: "No public money or other property shall be expended or appropriated for the use, benefit or maintenance of any religious institution or association."

The distinguishing principle of the "separation" tradition is that the state is required to refrain from involvement in religious activities and from support for religious organizations—which presently include once "nonreligious" Shinto institutions like Ise Shrine and Yasukuni Shrine. Moreover, the criteria that the government must use to assess the qualifications of organizations that apply for this status are clearly specified in terms that forbid violation of the constitutionally guaranteed principle of religious freedom.

The law that codifies the *seikyō bunri* tradition is the Religious Juridical Persons Law (*Shūkyō hōjin hō*).[16] Its aim is to provide qualified religious organizations with the legal right to possess, maintain, and dispose of property and to engage in business enterprises for the achievement of religious purposes. Religious organizations are legally free to exist whether or not they apply for religious juridical person status, but those which choose to do so gain certain tax advantages.[17] The task of determining whether an organization may be authorized as a religious juridical person remains a governmental function. But government officials, though responsible to authenticate information submitted by an organization applying for religious juridical person status, are legally prohibited from interfering in matters relating to creed, rules, customs, or religious activities. The law rests on, and implements, the constitutional principles of religious freedom and separation of religion and state.

---

[16] Chronologically, the first legal statute that codified the *seikyō bunri* tradition was the Religious Juridical Persons Ordinance (*Shūkyō hōjin rei*) of December 28, 1945. The Religious Juridical Persons Law (*Shūkyō hōjin hō*) went into effect on April 3, 1951.

The Religious Juridical Persons Ordinance was issued under the authority of the Occupation, but had no basis in Japanese law. It was inadequate, moreover, because it permitted religious organizations to receive juridical person status simply by filling out a registration form and filing it with the proper government office. This opened the door to a number of abuses.

The Religious Juridical Persons Law was issued under the authority of the Japanese government and was based on the 1947 Constitution, particularly the articles guaranteeing religious freedom and separation of religion and state.

Since the law was intended to correct defects in the ordinance and to uphold the same general orientation, I have chosen to ignore the difference between the two in this discussion and refer to both under the name Religious Juridical Persons Law.

[17] They are exempt from the juridical persons tax, real estate tax, and registration tax.

Both the Meiji Constitution of 1890 and the new Constitution of 1947 contain a guarantee of religious freedom. But if one takes it that the meaning of the 1890 guarantee is to the Religious Organizations Law as the meaning of the 1947 guarantee is to the Religious Juridical Persons Law, the two guarantees, however similar in form, turn out to be quite different in orientation and consequence.

A TENTATIVE CLASSIFICATION

As might have been expected, the 1945 shift to a legal code oriented to "separation" by no means spelled an end to the tradition of "unity." It did, however, strengthen the position of religious groups that had formerly been persecuted as illegal or that, in order to escape persecution, had taken refuge under the skirts of a recognized religious body. Some of these groups support the separation principle enunciated in the 1947 Constitution.

For the purpose of analysis, Japanese religious groups with an interest in political affairs can be divided into three classes. The first class is that of "traditional unity." Following from the tradition of *saisei itchi*, "traditional unity" suggests an integrated relationship between the world of politics and the world of religion. It includes the idea that religious organizations as such do not engage in political activity or present themselves as critics of government. As opposed to the anti-clericalism characteristic of relationships between church and state in some periods of Western history, the idea that the state is generally supportive of religion, and religion of the state, belongs to the concept of "traditional unity."

The second class is that of "anti-traditional unity." This term stands for the position that the security and prosperity of the nation, represented by the emperor and the government, depend on its conversion to and support for one particular form of religion. This position is best typified by the Nichiren Shōshū, which will be considered in some detail shortly.

The third class is that of "separation of religion and state."

In this case the state, though by no means hostile to religion, neither participates in religious activities nor supports religious institutions. By the same token, religious institutions refrain from direct involvement in politics — though they may seek to influence developments in the political realm through an intermediate organization of their own devising, as Risshō Kōseikai does through its World Conference on Religion and Peace.

If politically concerned religious groups are divided into these classes, the result looks something like that shown in table 6. The membership figures in table 6 must be taken cum grano salis for at least three reasons: (1) they are often general estimates, (2) most people are counted both as Shrine Shinto adherents and as adherents to some stream of Buddhism, with the consequence that some figures overlap, and (3) depending on the issue, many members of the two "unity" classes support separation of religion and state, and many members of the "separation" class support the tradition of unity. The table, therefore, should be taken as suggestive, not hard fact. But even when these qualifications are taken into account, the overwhelming numerical strength of organizations that generally support the traditional idea of politico-religious unity is indisputable.

The traditional unity, anti-traditional unity, and separation positions can be construed as the three main parameters in terms of which issues concerning religion and the state have taken shape in the postwar period.

GETTING DOWN TO CASES

Recent years have seen the emergence of a number of issues that have drawn the attention of scholars of Japanese religion and society. Among unresolved issues, the most prominent are: (1) the proposed legislation that would define Ise Shrine and Yasukuni Shrine as nonreligious institutions and support them with government funds, (2) the intention of the government to make it possible "without causing friction with neighboring countries" for the prime minister and other state ministers to pay official

TABLE 6
THREE CLASSES OF RELIGIOUS GROUPS

TRADITIONAL UNITY		ANTI-TRADITIONAL UNITY		SEPARATION	
Group	Members	Group	Members	Group	Members
		SHINTO *Shrine Shinto*			
Jinja Honchō	86,397,968	*Sect Shinto*			
Izumo Ōyashirokyō	1,167,577	Ōmoto	171,821	Konkōkyō	448,393
Kurozumikyō	295,225				
Misogikyō	100,610				
Ontakekyō	622,380				
		BUDDHISM *Nara Sects*			
Fudō Shū	1,623,551				
Others	774,953	*Tendai Sects*			
Tendai Shū	608,960				
Washū	100,750	*Shingon Sects*			
Kōyasan Shingon Shū	5,448,400				
Shingonshū Chizanha	1,536,987			Gedatsukai	238,222
Shingonshū Buzanha	1,186,978				
		Pure Land Sects			
				Jōdo Shinshū	
				Honganjiha	6,921,908
				Shinshū Ōtaniha	5,533,194
		Zen Sects			
Rinzaishū					
Myōshinjiha	1,216,680				
Sōtō Shū	6,935,814	*Nichiren Sects*			
Bussho Gonenkai					
Kyōdan	2,018,250	Nichiren Shōshū	17,736,757	Myōchikai Kyōdan	917,538
Nichiren Shū	2,672,904	[Sōka Gakkai]	[17,639,866]	Risshō Kōseikai	6,266,750
Reiyūkai	3,155,635				
		CHRISTIANITY			
				Catholic	397,043
				Orthodox	9,378
				Protestant	489,861
		OTHER			
Seichō no Ie	817,089			Ennōkyō	401,789
				PL Kyōdan	2,038,826
				Tenrikyō	1,777,144
Total	116,580,711		17,908,578		25,434,045

NOTE: Only organizations regarded as belonging to the three classes are included in this table. The figures indicate the number of adherents reported as of December 31, 1988 (*Shūkyō nenkan* 1990). Most Sōka Gakkai membership figures are included in those of the Nichiren Shōshū and thus do not enter into the total shown for the Anti-Traditional Unity class.

visits to Yasukuni Shrine and participate in Shinto rites there each year on the anniversary of the end of World War II, and (3) the lawsuit challenging the use of public funds for the Shinto rite known as the Daijōsai ("Great Food Offering Ceremony") following the enthronement ceremony in November 1990.[18]

Among the issues that have been resolved, four cases stand out: (1) a case involving the use of public funds for a Shinto-tradition rite, (2) a conflict involving Buddhism that was settled out of court, (3) two lawsuits protesting former prime minister Nakasone Yasuhiro's official visit to Yasukuni Shrine in 1985, and (4) a suit brought by the Christian wife of a deceased Self-Defense Forces officer protesting his enshrinement in the Yamaguchi Gokoku Shrine.[19]

The question to be considered here is whether analysis of the four resolved cases in terms of the "traditional unity," "anti-traditional unity," and "separation" parameters will make it possible to identify a direction or tendency. The result will be open-ended, subject to modification as other cases become available for analysis.

CASE 1. THE TSU CITY SUIT

The lawsuit over a Shinto rite began in 1965 in the city of Tsu when Sekiguchi Seiichi, a Communist member of the city council, charged that the mayor, Kakunaga Kiyoshi, had misused public funds by paying four Shinto priests an honorarium of ¥7,663 for conducting a *jichinsai* or "grounds-purification rite" prior to the construction of a municipal gymnasium. The ques-

---

[18] The Sokui-no-rei enthronement ceremony was held on November 12, 1990. The Daijōsai, widely reported in news media as a Shinto rite in which the emperor receives divine character, began on the evening of November 22 and ended before daybreak on November 23, 1990. For an instructive analysis of the Daijōsai problem from a Christian perspective, see Nishikawa Shigenori, "The Daijōsai, the Constitution, and Christian Faith," *Japan Christian Quarterly* 56/3 (1990): 132–46.

[19] A related issue is that of the era name (*gengō*). What was a bill at the time this inquiry was originally undertaken has now become a law. This law requires all institutions that serve the public to indicate dates not by means of the Western calendar but by means of the era name and year associated with a given emperor. The year 1989, for example, the first year in the reign of Emperor Akihito, is known as "Heisei 1," 1990 as "Heisei 2," etc.

tion was not whether the city could, even exceptionally, legally engage in a religious activity or use public funds for a religious purpose. It was understood by all concerned that the Constitution prohibits the former in Article 20, Section 3 and the latter in Article 89. The question was whether the Shinto rite was religious. If so, the city, represented by the mayor, was guilty of violating the Constitution. The case was tried in three courts.

The Tsu District Court decided in favor of the mayor in 1967. It maintained that the Shinto rite, though religious in origin, is now nothing but a convention. It found the use of public funds for this purpose "inappropriate, but not illegal."

The Nagoya High Court, in an appellate trial, reversed the decision of the lower court. In 1971 it held: (1) that Shrine Shinto, whether considered by scholars of religion or scholars of constitutional law, is clearly a religion, (2) that the rite for purifying the grounds is not a secular but a religious rite, and (3) that the mayor had violated Article 20, Section 3 of the Constitution.

The Supreme Court, in 1977, upheld the decision of the Tsu District Court. Basing their view of whether the rite was religious on what they called "the assessment of religion among ordinary people and the ideas current in [Japanese] society," the Supreme Court justices (ten out of fifteen) decided that since the Shinto rite was not intended to propagate Shintoism and since it did not interfere with other religions, it should be regarded not as a religious but as a secular (*sezokuteki*) activity. Consequently, the use of public funds to pay those who performed the rite was held not unconstitutional.

The Tsu City suit, since it marks *the first time that a case having to do with the principle of separation between religion and state has gone all the way to the Supreme Court,* is widely regarded among Japanese people as having great significance.

The Tsu City *jichinsai* decision stands not as an isolated event but as a precedent that will play an important role in the shaping of coming developments. Both supporters and opponents of the Supreme Court decision see it as guiding the resolution of pending issues. The *Jinja Shinpō*, for example, organ of the Jinja Honchō (Association of Shinto Shrines), hailed the decision as justifying official (rather than merely private) visits by prime ministers to Ise and Yasukuni Shrines and the performance of Shinto rites in the palace by the emperor.[20] The Roman Catholic Church, conversely, protested the decision as blurring the relationship between religion and state,[21] and the *Kirisuto Shinbun*, which often speaks for Japan's largest Protestant body, the United Church of Christ in Japan, observed that the decision signals "a dangerous trend."[22] To the extent that these assessments are correct, it follows that the more Shinto rites are defined as secular, the freer the government will be to link religious and political structures with a common orientation to the "traditional unity" form of the *saisei itchi* tradition.

CASE 2. SŌKA GAKKAI AND THE FREEDOM OF SPEECH ISSUE

If importance is weighed by the degree to which a religious organization's actions are watched and reacted to by other religious organizations, then Sōka Gakkai is clearly the most important organization on the religio-political scene in contemporary Japan. The story of its founding need not be repeated here, but it will be useful to review its position in the Japanese Buddhist world and some of the principles it advocates.

Sōka Gakkai is not a Buddhist sect. It is a lay association (one among others) of the sect known as the Nichiren Shōshū. The Nichiren Shōshū contends "that Nichiren is the true Buddha of the present age, that the state should build an ordination hall where properly qualified people may receive the Buddhist precepts and take on themselves the Buddhist discipline, and that the state should be governed by Buddhist principles. This last teaching, known in Japanese as *ōbutsu myōgō* . . . calls for a fusion of imperial authority and Buddhist institutions and includes the demand that Nichiren Buddhism be established as the state religion."[23] Sōka Gakkai, as a lay association under the Nichiren Shōshū, is presumably guided by essentially the same principles.

---

[20] *Shūmu Jihō*, no. 42 (March 1978): 11.
[21] *Katorikku Shinbun* (October 16, 1977).
[22] *Kirisuto Shinbun* (July 23, 1977).
[23] Matsuno Junkō, "Buddhist Sects," in Hori, *Japanese Religion*, 206–7.

Its proclivity for direct involvement in Japanese political affairs was more than hinted at by former President Ikeda Daisaku when he said in 1966, "Sōka Gakkai will enter into no political activities whatever *outside Japan*."[24]

Legally incorporated as an independent religious juridical person (*tan'i shūkyō hōjin*) in 1952, Sōka Gakkai soon entered the political arena. In 1956 it had three candidates elected to the House of Councilors (the upper house of the National Diet). In 1964 it established the Kōmeitō ("Clean Government Party") as its political arm, and this body, which in 1967 had twenty-five candidates elected to the House of Representatives, has now grown to be a respected, sometimes pivotal force in the Diet.[25]

It is against the background of these principles and developments that the issue concerning freedom of speech and press came to the fore.

In 1969 Fujiwara Hirotatsu, a political scientist and critic, sought to publish his book *Sōka Gakkai o kiru* [Beheading Sōka Gakkai]. As the title implies, the book is an indictment of Sōka Gakkai and what the author calls "its bastard," the Kōmeitō. The substance of his criticism is that Sōka Gakkai, pulling the strings of the Kōmeitō, is a Machiavellian organization that gives lip service to democratic principles but in fact relies on principles and methods that show it to be an enemy of democracy.

Sōka Gakkai, for its part, is oriented to the principle that the

---

[24] *Sōka Gakkai no rinen to jissen* [Sōka Gakkai in ideal and practice]. Tokyo Daigaku Hokekyō Kenkyūkai, ed. (Tokyo: Daisan Bunmeisha, 1975), 132. Emphasis added.

[25] With reference to the emergence of the Kōmeitō, Jan Swyngedouw observes: "It is this fact which dominates for a great part, if not completely, the political stance taken by Japan's other religious organizations" ("Japanese Religions and Party Politics: Some Recent Examples," *Japan Missionary Bulletin* 32 (1978): 543). Thus the liaison organization popularly known as Shinshūren (the abbreviation for *Shin Nihon Shūkyō Dantai Rengōkai*, the "Union of New Religious Organizations of Japan"), led by Risshō Kōseikai, has sought, without entering the field of politics directly, to establish ties with political power-holders and to exercise influence among conservative politicians and in elections. Since voters in the world of religious organizations, exclusive of Sōka Gakkai, are loosely estimated to number anywhere from five million to eight million, it is easy to see why the politicians, from their side, have been eager to cultivate religious organizations. (For a detailed account of politically active religious organizations and how they have fared in recent years in supporting candidates for political office, see Matsuo Yoshiyuki, "Sengo hoshu seiji to shūkyō kyōdan" [Postwar conservative politics and religious organizations], *Gendai no me* 19/3 (1978): 62–71.

important thing is to get people to believe and join the one, true religion: the form of Buddhism taught by the Nichiren Shōshū.[26] It holds that this is the way to personal and national well-being and that democratic principles will reach fulfillment only on this basis.

Whether Fujiwara's criticisms are, or were, accurate is not at issue. What is important, if one may judge from Fujiwara's report and from the subsequent actions of Sōka Gakkai and the Kōmeitō, is that various attempts, some apparently extra-legal, were made to prevent the publication of Fujiwara's book.[27]

In the end what was published was not only the book but also the story of the pressures that had been brought to bear — pressures widely interpreted as inimical to freedom of speech and press. The result was a great furor in the media, a public apology by the president of Sōka Gakkai, the resignation of a Kōmeitō figure, and an allegedly "more complete" separation between Sōka Gakkai and the Kōmeitō.

In brief, then, the points to be considered are these: (1) the principles of the Nichiren Shōshū, (2) Sōka Gakkai's comparatively direct involvement in politics through the Kōmeitō up to the time of the Fujiwara incident, and (3) its subsequent "retreat" from politics.

The first point to note is that Nichiren Shōshū principles, in and of themselves, have direct and straightforward political implications. If Sōka Gakkai, in acting to realize those principles, were not bound by other constraints, there would appear to be no intrinsic reason to establish the Kōmeitō at all, let alone to pronounce it, after 1970, more autonomous. The external constraints in this case appear to be twofold: the Constitution, which requires that "no religious organization shall . . . exercise any political authority" (Art. 20, Section 1), and media-represented popular sentiment, which in this case took the form of expressions of outrage at the violation of rights held essential to

---

[26] Ikeda Daisaku, *Seiji to shūkyō* [Politics and religion] (Tokyo: Otori Shoin, 1964), 203; *Seiji to shūkyō* [Politics and religion], rev. ed. (Tokyo: Ushio Shuppansha, 1969), 162.

[27] Cf. James W. White, *The Sokagakkai and Mass Society* (Stanford, California: Stanford University Press, 1970), 345–46.

democracy and guaranteed by the Constitution.[28] It appears, therefore, that the changes under consideration were in fact externally occasioned.

The internal corollary is that the more Sōka Gakkai is guided by power considerations, that is, the more it seeks not merely to influence politicians but, through the Kōmeitō, to acquire and exercise political power, the more it must accommodate itself to prevailing currents and run the risk of diverging from the principles espoused by its parent organization.[29] Thus its actions on behalf of the principles are vulnerable to two damaging interpretations: they can be viewed either as a watering down of Nichiren Shōshū principles or as a matter of concealing these principles behind tactical professions of loyalty to other, more generally accepted principles. The first entails severe tension with the parent organization, the second, widespread feelings of skepticism and suspicion among the general public. This is, in fact, the continuing predicament of Sōka Gakkai.

Sōka Gakkai is the main proponent of "anti-traditional unity," but insofar as this case is concerned, it is evident that there has been little if any progress toward realizing its idea of the proper relationship between religion and state.

CASE 3. THE NAKASONE SHRINE VISIT

In 1985 Nakasone Yasuhiro participated in Shinto rites at Yasukuni Shrine in his official capacity as prime minister. Because of strong, angry protests from neighboring countries in Asia, especially China and South Korea,[30] the prime ministers who suc-

---

[28] Article 21 of the Constitution reads: "Freedom of assembly and association as well as speech, press, and all other forms of expression are guaranteed."

[29] Since 1970, the Kōmeitō has omitted from its statement of principles the phrase *buppō minshū*, which in paraphrase means something like "one people under the universal principle of Buddhism." Ikeda Daisaku, president of Sōka Gakkai from 1960 to 1979 and since 1975 president of Sōka Gakkai International, has long insisted that Sōka Gakkai has "no intention of becoming a state religion" and that it stands by the principle of religious freedom for both true and false religions (Ikeda, *Seiji to shūkyō* [Politics and religion], rev. ed., 203).

[30] In these countries Yasukuni Shrine is still viewed as a symbol of Japanese militarism. A small proportion of Japanese people share this view, but the vast majority

ceeded him have refrained from official visits to the shrine. The government clearly intends, however, to reinstitute this custom as soon as it is diplomatically feasible.[31] In order to do so, it needs to establish that official participation in Shinto rites at Yasukuni Shrine on the part of cabinet ministers does not violate the Constitution.

In November 1989 the Osaka District Court rejected a ¥6 million damage suit filed by six people who claimed that Nakasone's official visit to Yasukuni Shrine in 1985 violated the constitutional provision requiring separation of religion and state. The presiding judge, Matsuo Masayuki, ruled that Nakasone visited the shrine to pay tribute to victims of World War II,

---

see it as a now-traditional place for honoring members of the Japanese armed forces who died during the Pacific War—indeed during all wars since 1868. For more on Yasukuni Shrine, see below, n. 33.

[31] In August 1990 the government announced its intention to establish a panel to discuss ways for cabinet ministers to pay annual visits to Yasukuni Shrine on August 15, the anniversary of the end of World War II, without eliciting the disapproval of neighboring countries. The panel is to include academics and intellectuals and submit a report to the cabinet secretary by the summer of 1991. On receiving the report, the government will publish its official view on the question of such visits to Yasukuni Shrine.

This seemingly plausible procedure, however, has a fatal flaw: the official view of the government on the question of official visits by cabinet members to Yasukuni Shrine has already been published—and was arrived at in much the same way. A fifteen-member advisory committee was convened by the cabinet secretary in August 1984, held twenty-one hearings during the next twelve months, and on August 9, 1985 presented a report indicating that the committee had split three ways: some favoring cabinet tribute at Yasukuni Shrine, some opposing it, and still others advocating the construction of a new, religiously neutral memorial for the war dead. Ignoring this split, the government announced its "conclusion": "Based upon the findings of this advisory committee, the government intends to take appropriate measures toward formal tribute by the cabinet at the Yasukuni Shrine." (Cited in Helen Hardacre, *Shintō and the State, 1868–1988* [Princeton: Princeton University Press, 1989], 151.) The Nakasone cabinet's official visit to Yasukuni Shrine took place just six days after the presentation of the report.

One would have to be gullible in the extreme not to recognize the new panel for what it is: a staged set of hearings that will allow academics and intellectuals to present an honest statement of their views, after which government leaders will claim that after examining all sides of the question, they have reasonably concluded that cabinet visits to Yasukuni Shrine are not unconstitutional—the very position taken by the government long before it established the panel!

On the government's use of hearings in order to define the Daijōsai or "Great Food Offering Ceremony" as a public function, cf. Nishikawa, "The Daijōsai," 133–35.

Photo 1: *Yasukuni Shrine*

not to infringe on the separation provision. He further ruled that since Nakasone's visit did not result in disadvantageous treatment of the plaintiffs in the area of faith or lead to the imposition of religious beliefs, they were not entitled to government compensation.

In December 1989 the Fukuoka District Court rejected a similar lawsuit: a ¥4.3 million damage suit filed against the government by forty-three citizens who, led by Buddhist priest Gunjima Tsuneaki, claimed that since Yasukuni is a Shinto shrine, Nakasone's official visit to Yasukuni Shrine in 1985 violated Article 20 of the Constitution. The ruling judge, Tomita Ikuo, interpreted Article 20 as giving citizens the right to adhere to any religion. Nakasone's visit, he said, did not infringe on this right. Consequently, there was no basis for compensation.

What stands out in these two rulings is the point that "separation" issues have been reduced to "religious freedom" issues. Unless coercion can be proved, there is no religious freedom issue, and if there is no religious freedom issue, there is no separation issue. This argument recurs in the next case.

CASE 4. ENSHRINEMENT OF A SELF-DEFENSE FORCES OFFICER

The tangled story of the enshrinement of a Self-Defense Forces officer, of the lawsuit brought by his Christian wife, and of the decisions handed down by various courts between 1979 and 1988 has been told many times.[32] Here a brief summary must suffice.

In 1968 Nakaya Takafumi died in a traffic accident while on active duty in the Self-Defense Forces. Not long afterward, the prefectural Veterans Association asked his widow, Nakaya Yasuko, for a copy of the death certificate so that they could proceed to enshrine his spirit in the Yamaguchi Gokoku Shrine. (*Gokoku* 護国 means "defending the country." All *gokoku* shrines are of the Shinto tradition and in the public mind are linked with Yasukuni Shrine.)[33]

Her husband was not a Christian, but Yasuko had already had her husband's ashes interred in her church ossuary and insisted that he was under the care of her church. She refused to turn over any documents or agree to the idea of enshrinement, saying, "As a Christian, I cannot accept deification of my husband by another religion."

In 1972, however, the Veterans Association, with documents supplied by the Self-Defense Forces, had the enshrinement (*gōshi*) carried out over her protests not only for her husband but also for twenty-six other men who had died while on active duty.[34] In

---

[32] A clear account may be found in Hardacre, *Shintō and the State*, 153–57.

[33] Before 1868, the various districts throughout Japan had their own shrines for remembering those who had fallen in battle. In 1868, these shrines were officially designated *shōkonsha* 招魂社 (literally, "shrines for invoking the spirits"). What is today known as Yasukuni Shrine began in 1869 as one of these *shōkonsha*. In 1879 it received the name "Yasukuni Shrine," and in 1939, the year Hitler invaded Poland and World War II began, all the *shōkonsha* except Yasukuni Shrine were renamed "*gokoku* shrines."

[34] The word *gōshi* 合祀 , usually translated "enshrinement," is defined in the authoritative Japanese dictionary *Kōjien* as "to enshrine two or more kami in a single shrine." The tricky word here is the verb. In English "to enshrine" means little more than "to cherish" or, more literally, "to enclose in a shrine." The Japanese word *matsuru* 祭る , however, is considerably more substantial. *Kōjien* gives three meanings: (1) to console a divine spirit (*shinrei* 神霊 , which can also be translated "the soul of a dead person") by means of offerings and instrumental music; (2) to reverence something or someone as a kami at a specific place dedicated to that purpose; to enshrine

1973, therefore, she sued the state, specifically its agency the Yamaguchi Prefectural Branch of the Self-Defense Forces, and the prefectural Veterans Association for violating the constitutional provision requiring separation of state and religion and for violating her right to religious freedom.

The case was first tried in the Yamaguchi District Court. In 1979 the presiding judge, Yokobatake Norio, ruled on the one hand that since the Veterans Association received assistance from the Self-Defense Forces in proceeding with the matter, the enshrinement did indeed violate the Constitution, Article 20 (the article that prohibits the state and its agencies from engaging in any religious act).

On the other hand, he ruled that religious freedom is guaranteed not only for the plaintiff but also for the defendants, and that since nobody had imposed their beliefs on the widow or forced her to pay homage to the soul of her husband at the shrine, neither the state nor the Veterans Association was in violation of the constitutional provision guaranteeing religious freedom. In view of the violation of Article 20, however, he ordered the state and the Veterans Association to pay the widow a solatium of ¥1 million plus five percent interest per year for the six-year period between the time the widow first appeared in court and the time a ruling had been handed down. Attorneys for the defendants appealed the ruling.

In June 1982 the Hiroshima High Court handed down a second ruling. In a word, it upheld the ruling of the lower court. Again, the attorneys for the defense appealed to a higher court.

The decision of the Supreme Court was handed down on June 1, 1988. It held, first of all, that the Veterans Association had acted alone when it engaged in the religious activity of enshrinement. Since the Veterans Association, despite its close links with the Self-Defense Forces, is not an agency of the state,

a kami; and (3) to pray. The second meaning seems most appropriate in this case.

Hardacre's translation of *gōshi* as "apotheosis" (*Shintō and the State*, 153) emphasizes the divine status attributed to the spirits of the dead in consequence of the enshrinement ritual. The usual translation "enshrinement" emphasizes the ritual act of enshrining two or more kami at a specific location. Neither translation quite captures both emphases. I use "enshrinement" only because this is the more generally employed term.

there was, the court found, no violation of Article 20 of the Constitution.

The Supreme Court went on to say, moreover, that even if the Self-Defense Forces were to have been found engaging in unconstitutional religious activity, the state is not to be held accountable unless coercion is involved.[35]

Finally, in answer to Nakaya Yasuko's claim that her "religious human rights" had been violated, the court held that when religious actions conflict and the differing parties have recourse to law, the legal proceedings may in fact violate the religious freedom of one party. In such a case, the injured party is advised to be "tolerant." At this point, then, the court was not so much establishing a legal precedent as reinforcing a moral view widely held in Japan, namely, that to suppress personal religious claims in the interest of community harmony is more virtuous than to insist on any purported "religious human rights." Conformity for the sake of harmony is the rule.

Nakaya Yasuko was ordered to repay the ¥1 million with interest.

THE TENDENCY EVIDENT IN THESE CASES

With regard to the question of how Japanese religious organizations line up on the relationship of religion and state, it was found that insofar as religious organizations have made their positions known, they can be divided into three classes: traditional unity, anti-traditional unity, and separation. The first has a history of nearly two thousand years, the second a history of nearly eight hundred years, and the last a history of less than fifty years. The separation principle is written into the Constitution, but the traditional unity orientation (modified by the anti-traditional unity orientation) is deeply rooted in the culture. The question arises, therefore, whether these prominent cases involving religion during the last thirty-five years give evidence of a tendency toward any one of these three orientations.

Anti-traditional unity is best represented by Sōka Gakkai.

---

[35] Hardacre, *Shintō and the State*, 156.

But the freedom of speech case in which Sōka Gakkai was involved can hardly be seen as a victory for the anti-traditional unity orientation. At best it was a standoff.

The traditional unity and the separation positions have encountered one another in three contests. The important question here, however, is not "Which side won?" but "What precedents have been established?"

In the Tsu City case, the Supreme Court found that the "grounds purification rite" was no longer religious. By implication this means that so long as "religion" is defined in terms of the individual and the faith-community, any rites conducted by community representatives and the natural community can be characterized as secular. This leaves the state free to establish links with "nonreligious" Shinto in accordance with the traditional unity orientation.

In the Nakasone shrine visit case, the courts dealt with the separation issue in two ways: by referring to the intention of the prime minister (his intention was not to violate the separation provision but to pay tribute to members of the armed forces who died for their country), and by referring to the principle of non-coercion (where there is no coercion, there is no infringement of the right of Japanese citizens to belong to any religion they choose). In principle this establishes that the prime minister, and by extension any servant of the state, is free to participate in any religious rite so long as there is no "intention" to violate the separation provision and so long as there is no coercion of other people. It is hard to imagine a more loosely conceived legal precedent, or one more advantageous to those who favor not separation of religion and state but some form of traditional unity.

The Nakaya case established one more precedent: the state is not in violation of the Constitution, even when performing unconstitutional religious activities, unless it coerces individuals to perform a religious activity or otherwise limits their religious freedom. In other words, when a violation of the constitutional principle of separation of religion and state is at issue, the question of violation of principle is reduced to the question of violation of the religious freedom of the individual. If coercion is not involved, the state is free to engage in some degree of religious activity.

All in all, there is a clear and unmistakable tendency at work in these cases. Legal precedents that support anti-traditional unity are non-existent. Legal precedents in support of separation of religion and state are found in some of the lower court rulings but in none of the Supreme Court rulings. Every case that has gone as far as the Supreme Court has resulted in a legal precedent that buttresses the traditional unity position.

GAZING INTO THE FUTURE

It may seem surprising that the Japanese public does not protest against this legal erosion of constitutional principle. The fact is, however, that these rulings have caused only small and short-lived ripples on the surface of what the novelist Endō Shūsaku calls the "swamp" of Japanese society.

The tradition with the longest history, the one that most people take for granted and would scarcely dream of questioning, calls for the unity of religion and state. It seems unlikely that we will soon see any radical change in this tradition. One can imagine, however, two circumstances that might strengthen the social and cultural rootage of the separation principle among Japanese people.

The first is external. Neighboring countries in Asia have already made strong protests about official cabinet visits to Yasukuni Shrine. Their protests are heard in Japan, it seems, not as calls to attend to principle but as emotional reactions from persons who remember how their people suffered under Japanese military power. On the Japanese government side, the hope is apparently that by offering apologies and by building bridges of trust and trade, these emotional reactions can be toned down. Japanese government leaders will then be free to do what their constituents expect: to pay ritual tribute to military personnel who died for emperor and country. But if the people of other nations, both through their governments and through non-governmental organizations, respond vigorously to Japanese court decisions on religion and state issues, constantly calling attention to questions of principle, this is bound to have an effect. Japanese people, including politicians, are extraordinarily sensitive to how they stand in the eyes of the world. Initially, responses from abroad will no doubt meet with attempts to work out a "political solution," but in the long run questions of principle cannot be evaded. External pressures can help stimulate reflection and discussion on the foundations and implications of the principle of separation of religion and state.

Without internal pressures, however, external pressures may easily give rise to anti-foreign nationalism. Where such internal pressures must come from is perhaps not entirely self-evident. The suggestion to be made here is that it can most naturally come from the tradition within which the separation principle first took shape, namely, the Christian tradition. At first glance it may seem implausible to expect effective pressure of any kind from the infinitesimal and divided Christian group, many of whose members implicitly accept the traditional unity position.[36]

But two facts are important in this context. First, it is undeniable that in the past, Christian persons, teachings, and institutions have helped to reshape Japanese society. This is particularly evident in women's education, in the passage of the anti-prostitution law, etc. — structures now taken for granted as a natural part of Japanese society. It should not be assumed, therefore, that Japan is impervious to Christian influence. Second, it is also undeniable that there is a sizable gap between the few Japanese Christians who have studied and understand the foundations of the separation principle and the majority who have not and do not. This means that it is essential for Japanese Christianity to draw on the experience and wisdom of those who have studied these matters and increase among its own members an understanding of the separation principle and of its meaning for democratic procedure. Printed materials produced for this purpose would naturally come to the attention of interested parties outside the church and could prove a productive stimulus

---

[36] See chap. 6, n. 15.

to reflection on the reasons underlying the separation principle and on the question of its contemporary application in Japan. A few Japanese Christian leaders are already calling for commitment to this immense, long-range educational task.[37] Whether it will materialize remains to be seen, but it seems clear that without some such effort, the future of the Japanese constitutional principle of separation of religion and state will remain bleak.

At bottom, however, the tension between the unity tradition and the separation tradition stems from the unresolved question of the relationship between two ways of being religious: the way that takes for granted the priority of the natural community, relegating personal religion to the category of taste and preference; and the way that takes for granted the priority of the faith-community, relegating the religion of natural community to secondary status. In the Constitution, the second understanding of religion seems to be the basic guide, but in Japanese culture as a whole, the first understanding is the basic fact. Because of this incongruence, court rulings on the relationship of religion and state have tended to erode constitutional principle in favor of cultural tradition. It seems likely that this trend will continue for the foreseeable future.

---

[37] One thinks, for example, of Ohki Hideo and the late Sacon Kiyoshi of Tokyo Union Theological Seminary, of Sasakawa Norikatsu and Mogami Toshiki of International Christian University, and of Nishikawa Shigenori, Director of the National Council for Monitoring Violations of the Separation of Religion and State. (I am grateful to David L. Swain for calling some of these names to my attention.)

Chapter 3

Reflections on the Path to Understanding in Religious Studies

P ROFESSOR YANAGAWA KEIICHI'S retirement from the University of Tokyo Department of Religious Studies in 1986 marked the end of an era.[1] As one of his former students, and as one deeply conscious of his continuing influence, I want to reflect on the nature of the religious studies enterprise in Japan during the last quarter-century, the period during which Professor Yanagawa taught at the University of Tokyo.

The general subject to be considered is "the study of religion and society in contemporary Japan." What I have in mind is not a general survey of the kinds of research that have been carried out during the last twenty-five years, but an analysis of the epistemological premises of the discipline.

Methodological reflection that focuses on the question of epistemology is a somewhat less than popular theme in religious studies publications in Japan. A hasty review of the materials published in *Shūkyō kenkyū* [Journal of religious studies] during

---

[1] This chapter originally appeared as one of a collection of articles presented in tribute to Professor Yanagawa on the occasion of his retirement from the University of Tokyo. Yanagawa Keiichi passed away in April, 1990.

the past decade shows that of some 1,800 lectures, articles, and research reports, only fifteen were devoted to methodological issues. Moreover, when methodological issues are under discussion, they most often take the form of discussions concerning the definition of religion. Discussions of the epistemological premises of the discipline are extremely rare.

The reason for this hesitance to come to grips with a problem of such fundamental importance is probably related to the notion of "academic territory." Epistemology has traditionally been relegated to the philosophers. "If there is an epistemological problem, let the philosophers solve it. Meanwhile, let's get on with our work." This robust, pragmatic attitude is the one that prevails. And it is manifestly true that one can carry out significant research without waiting around for an epistemological problem to be identified and resolved. To refrain from research until every methodological issue has been satisfactorily put to rest would lead to numbness and paralysis.

At issue here, however, is not the question of epistemology in general, but the question of the epistemological premises of the discipline of religious studies as practiced in Japan today. Just as "war is too important to leave to the generals," so this question is too important to leave to the philosophers. Like other academic disciplines, religious studies aims at increase of knowledge. It is essential, therefore, that it be as clear as possible about its path to knowledge.

The present essay does not pretend to achieve this clarity. It has the more modest aim of calling attention to the issue and inviting further reflection.

ANALYSIS

To the best of my knowledge there is only one discussion of religious studies methodology that is generally regarded as normative in Japan. This is the discussion presented by Kishimoto Hideo in his frequently reprinted book *Shūkyōgaku* [Religious studies].[2] As Chairman of the Department of Religious

---

[2] Tokyo: Taimeidō, 1961.

Studies at the University of Tokyo until his death in 1964, Kishimoto was a man of considerable influence, and with particular regard to the matter of religious studies methodology, his influence remains strong.

In this book Kishimoto initiates his discussion of methodology by identifying four types of academic discipline that deal with religion: philosophy of religion, theology, history of religion, and religious studies. In the broad sense of the term, he tells us, "religious studies" includes all four types. Then he proceeds to narrow down the sense in which the term is to be understood. First he distinguishes two kinds of academic orientation characteristic of these four types: a normative orientation and a descriptive. For objective scholarship the descriptive orientation is deemed normative (no pun intended). Consequently he rules out the two disciplines described as intentionally normative: philosophy of religion and theology. Further distinguishing between historical and systematic studies, he takes the latter as his guide and thus rules out history of religion. This leaves religious studies in the narrow sense of the term. Embracing phenomenology of religion, religious anthropology, religious geography, sociology of religion, psychology of religion, etc., it is essentially a systematic discipline. As Wakimoto Tsuneya says, "This way of dividing things up may seem a bit schematic, but on the whole, these are the classifications generally acknowledged in the world of [religious studies] scholarship."[3]

This characterization of religious studies is accompanied by a specific ideal: the discipline and those who pursue it are to be "objective." A distinction is drawn between subject and object, and we learn (largely by indirection) that being objective means to restrict oneself to describing facts and analyzing their interconnections. The scholar is to be dispassionate, disinterested. Kishimoto's advice as to how to be objective has never been put in writing so far as I know, but tradition has it that he said, "When you choose a religious phenomenon to study, decide on one that you are not affiliated with." This pragmatic rule has

---

[3] Wakimoto Tsuneya, "Shūkyōgaku" [Religious studies], in Oguchi Iichi and Hori Ichirō, eds., *Shūkyōgaku jiten* [Dictionary of religious studies] (Tokyo: Tokyo Daigaku Shuppankai, 1973): 269.

been a helpful guide for many. On the whole, it has probably strengthened the normative view that religious studies is to be objective. Yet it also suggests a problem of considerable importance.

It might seem that Kishimoto's emphasis on objectivity rests on a firm and unshakable dichotomy between the observing subject who can safely be ignored and the observed object that is alone worthy of study. On this view the question of the role of the subject in coming to know the object simply does not arise. In fact the question is largely tabooed because it seems to open the door to uncontrollable subjectivity. But reading between the lines, one can see that the question of the role of the subject had to be dealt with, at least in a minimal way, even from the outset. Otherwise there would have been no necessity for the pragmatic rule that tradition has preserved. This matter will call for further attention shortly.

In essentials, however, it is probably fair to describe Kishimoto's epistemological premises as stemming from the intellectual tradition that traces its origins to Comtean positivism. To be sure, Kishimoto does not speak of a three-stage law of intellectual development, nor does he envision research results presented in the form of mathematical formulas. Consequently he cannot be identified as a doctrinaire positivist. He would not acknowledge the "I am a camera" position put forward by at least one recent advocate of the positivist outlook. Yet for all its "softness," Kishimoto's epistemological position can definitely be identified as basically positivistic. It is a position that would be inconceivable without the influence of Auguste Comte.

The guidelines offered by Kishimoto thirty years ago have become, over the years, almost unquestionable principles. The only significant modification that has come to my attention has to do with the role of the subject in the pursuit of knowledge. Particularly for those engaged in research that involved them with living people whose cooperation could be won only by a deliberate effort to establish rapport and whose actions and attitudes were clearly influenced to some degree by the presence of the person or persons conducting the research, it became impossible to avoid assigning some role to the subject. For the purpose of role-assignment, a convenient phrase was tucked into the methodological sections of research reports: the phrase "participant-observer." This phrase seemed to offer a happy solution to the problem of how to clarify the role of the subject in relation to the object. In reality, however, it simply offered a way of acknowledging the existence of the problem and seeming to come to grips with it while actually avoiding it.

In recent years there have been a few efforts to reopen questions of methodology, particularly as a result of encounters with philosophically inclined sociologists like Thomas Luckmann, with positivistically inclined sociologists like Bryan Wilson, and with socially committed sociologists like Robert Bellah and Peter Berger (whatever the differences in the content of their commitments). For the most part, however, these efforts have yet to bear fruit.

I think it correct to say that most people engaged in the study of religion and society in contemporary Japan continue to be oriented by the schematic guidelines laid down by Kishimoto thirty years ago. The subject / object dichotomy remains intact, modified only by compromising phrases like "participant-observer" and "sympathetic detachment."

ASSESSMENT

It has long been recognized that significant research can be conducted even on the basis of mistaken theoretical principles. Probably nobody alive today would wish to defend Durkheim's notion of totemism or his view of its role in the evolution of religion. Yet there is probably nobody alive today who would claim that Durkheim's contributions to the study of religion and society are insignificant or unworthy of the attention of present-day scholars.

By the same token, it has to be recognized that significant research can be (and has been) conducted on the basis of dubious epistemological principles. The high quality of Japanese language publications in religious studies speaks for itself. I often wish that Western scholars could avail themselves of Japanese publications as readily as Japanese scholars make use of Western works. (How fine it would be if there were a computerized database whereby people could gain access to abstracts and perhaps even to translations of works published in Japanese!)

It must be admitted, however, that a reassessment of Kishimoto's guidelines is long overdue. It is quite surprising, actually, that his schema for classifying and characterizing the types of disciplines for which the study of religious phenomena is central has not, in Japan, led to rigorous questioning of the basis on which these classifications were made or of the epistemological premises they serve.

Yet with the recognition that these premises derive from the positivist tradition, one is also made aware that this tradition is in principle unable to provide a satisfactory answer to the question of the role of the subject in the process of knowledge.

In practice we have come to recognize that human perceptions interact with "data" to shape our cognitions — not only in the world at large but also in the world of scholarship, the human and natural sciences alike.[4] In the world of religious studies, however, we have yet to incorporate this recognition into our frame of reference.[5] The question of how to do so is probably the most critical methodological issue that confronts religious studies in Japan today.

THE WAY AHEAD

An essential part of these reflections is to consider what resources offer promise of helpfulness with regard to this methodological issue. Perhaps it would be best to begin by identifying a line of

---

[4] For the natural sciences, see Garu Zukav, *The Dancing Wu Li Masters: An Overview of the New Physics* (Great Britain: Fontana Paperbacks, 1980), Martin Gardner, *The Ambidextrous Universe: Mirror Asymmetry and Time-reversed Worlds*, 2nd ed. (New York: Penguin Books, 1979), and Heinz R. Pagels, *The Cosmic Code: Quantum Physics as the Language of Nature* (Toronto and New York: Bantam Books, 1983).

[5] For an argument in favor of the positivistic position evident in the work of Bryan Wilson, see Akaike Noriaki, "Sympathetic Understanding and Objective Observation," *Japanese Journal of Religious Studies* 9 (1982): 53–64. For an opposing argument, see Araki Michio, "Toward an Integrated Understanding of Religion and Society: Hidden Premises in the Scientific Apparatus of the Study of Religion," *Japanese Journal of Religious Studies* 9 (1982): 65–76.

thought that does not promise to be helpful. I refer to the question of how to define religion.

Nobody is more keenly aware of the immense variety of definitions of religion than those engaged in religious studies. When it comes to definitions of religion, we suffer an *embarras de richesses*. Theistic definitions, atheistic definitions, substantive definitions, functional definitions, visible religion, invisible religion, civil religion—one hardly knows which way to turn. Moreover, unless some definition is adopted, one cannot even get started. Since there is no question of attributing exclusive validity to any one definition, we generally have recourse to the necessary expedient of classifying the definition we frame as a "working definition." This gets us off the hook. Though admittedly arbitrary, this classification has the virtue of sounding modest and allows us to get on with our task. It allows us to avoid getting bogged down inextricably in the definitional problem.

If what is required is a definition of religion that can be applied universally without reference to space or time and that will commend itself persuasively to scholars of every perspective, then the problem of definition is probably insoluble. The best we can hope for is the working definition whereby we stake out in a general way the type of religious phenomenon that we choose to study.

With particular reference to the epistemological issue concerning the interaction of subject and object in the knowledge process, it seems self-evident that defining and redefining the object, no matter how precisely, cannot lead to a resolution of the matter. What is required is an epistemological perspective that will help us not to dichotomize subject and object but to take into account the role of the cognizing subject and hence of the world view, categories, and values by means of which we perceive, analyze, and understand.

This is not a plea for the legitimacy of unbridled subjectivity. It is a call for recognition of the fact that the observing subject is not a mere camera but a human being with a world view, categories, and values that shape and inform what he or she "sees." This implies the possibility that people raised in different cultures and employing different categories may see the same thing in different ways—or see different things entirely. We need, therefore, an epistemological perspective that will allow us to take such differences into account. The task of developing a meta-language may be beyond us just now, but we can get on with the task of reflection on the role that our world views, categories, and values play in shaping and informing our perspectives. This includes the question of the "malleability" of categories, values, and world views both with regard to comprehending thought-worlds initially alien to us and with regard to communicating what we learn to people of our own or another culture.

One line of thought with resources relevant to this task is the American line that runs through Norman Brown, Clifford Geertz, Robert Bellah, and Paul Rabinow.[6] Another is the European line that runs through Edmund Husserl, Alfred Schutz and Maurice Natanson, and Thomas Luckmann.[7] Common to both is a denial that scientific knowledge based on a supposed opposition between subject and object is the ultimate form of

---

[6] Norman O. Brown, *Love's Body* (New York: Alfred A. Knopf and Random House, 1966); Clifford Geertz, *The Interpretation of Cultures* (New York: Basic Books, 1973); Robert N. Bellah, *Beyond Belief: Essays on Religion in a Post-traditional World* (New York: Harper and Row, 1970); Paul Rabinow, *Reflections on Fieldwork in Morocco* (Berkeley and Los Angeles: University of California Press, 1977). See also Paul Rabinow and William M. Sullivan, eds., *Interpretive Social Science: A Reader* (Berkeley: University of California Press, 1979); Stephen A. Tyler, *Cognitive Anthropology* (New York: Holt, Rinehart and Winston, 1969); Gregory Bateson, *Naven: A Survey of the Problems Suggested by a Composite Picture of the Culture of a New Guinea Tribe Drawn from Three Points of View*, 2nd ed. (Stanford, California: Stanford University Press, 1958) and *Steps to an Ecology of Mind* (San Francisco: Chandler Publications, 1970); and Morris Berman, *The Reenchantment of the World* (Toronto and New York: Bantam Books, 1981).

[7] Edmund Husserl, *The Crisis of European Sciences and Transcendental Phenomenology*, transl. by David Carr (Evanston, Illinois: Northwestern University Press, 1970); Alfred Schutz, *Collected Papers I: The Problem of Social Reality*, ed. by Maurice Natanson (The Hague: Martinus Nijhoff, 1962), *The Phenomenology of the Social World*, transl. by George Walsh and Frederick Lehnert (London: Heinemann Educational Books, 1967), *Collected Papers II: Studies in Social Theory*, ed. by Arvid Brodersen (The Hague: Martinus Nijhoff, 1976), and *Collected Papers III: Studies in Phenomenological Philosophy*, ed. by I. Schutz (The Hague: Martinus Nijhoff, 1975); Maurice Natanson, ed., *Phenomenology and Social Reality: Essays in Memory of Alfred Schutz* (The Hague: Martinus Nijhoff, 1970); Thomas Luckmann, *Life-World and Social Realities* (London: Heinemann Educational Books, 1983).

human knowledge. Both seek to locate the knower in a cultural matrix, a shared world of meaning. Both insist that the path to knowledge they discern is more in accord with reality, hence more scientific, than positivist objectivism. The difference between the two lines is that the American line is primarily associated with literature, psychology, sociology, and anthropology, whereas the European line is more closely associated with philosophy and sociology. It would be quite possible, however, to consider them as a single line of varied resources.

There may be yet other lines of thought in Japan or elsewhere with which I am unacquainted. If so, I trust that somebody will be kind enough to enlighten me. In any case there is a growing body of thought to which we can turn. I venture to hope that study groups will be formed and their deliberations made available for the benefit of all.

Positivistic assumptions have so thoroughly permeated modern education and modern scholars' views of proper scientific method that it is difficult for us to adopt different epistemological assumptions, even when we have learned to become critical of those by which we continue to be guided. We are at home with the subject/object dichotomy and were nursed on the notion that only research which focuses on the object can be "objective." It seems obvious, until we learn otherwise, that research which includes a conscious effort to identify the role of the cognizing subject is bound to be "subjective." And in fact efforts of this kind are not infrequently vulnerable to this charge—a perhaps inevitable consequence of seeking to refashion the epistemological universe in which we "live and move and have our being." Yet the negative resonances that accompany the word "subjective" must not deter us from recognizing that this once so obvious assessment often reflects an implicit reliance on the positivistic epistemology. If it is important, as I believe it is, to account for the role of the cognizing subject in the process of cognition, it follows that we must make the effort, however few the guidelines, to come to a new understanding of the path to understanding in religious studies.

The positivistic schema, despite its substantial contribution to the development of high-caliber religious studies in Japan,

will have to be replaced. The transition will doubtless be fraught
with uncertainties and tensions, but given increasing awareness
of the fundamental importance of the problem, this transition
can be avoided only at the cost of imperilling the logical integrity
of the discipline.

Part 2

Studies in

Japanese Christianity

Chapter 4

Secularization Theory and Japanese Christianity

MUCH OF THE FASCINATION—and aversion—felt for the term "secularization" appears to stem from its very ambiguity. Few terms employed in scholarly inquiry can have carried such diametrically opposed meanings. On the one hand, it is used to indicate the decline of religious beliefs and influence in a population formerly deemed religious. On the other, it is used to refer to a reorientation of religious concerns from the next world to this—and thus to the emergence of a new form of religious belief and influence. If it used in a value-neutral way, it is also used in a value-laden way as something to abhor or celebrate—even as part of an ideology of history. The question has been raised whether such a multivalent term can have any positive role to play in scientific discourse without rigorous purgation. Yet for all its diverse and sometimes mutually opposed meanings, we cannot seem to leave it alone. As to a dental cavity, we keep coming back to it, probing it, hoping it will clear up or go away.

This particular study has a very limited aim: to see if secularization theory can help clarify what has been happening in recent years in Japanese Christianity as exemplified by the Nihon Kirisuto Kyōdan (United Church of Christ in Japan).

Before this matter can be explored, however, it will be necessary to do three things: (1) to specify why I have chosen to focus on the Nihon Kirisuto Kyōdan, (2) to offer a working definition of the terms "religious" and "secular," and (3) to indicate what is here meant by "secularization theory."

PRELIMINARY CONSIDERATIONS

WHY THE NIHON KIRISUTO KYŌDAN?

The decision to focus on the Nihon Kirisuto Kyōdan derives not from the notion that it is somehow a "representative sample" of Japanese Christianity as a whole. Such an assertion could hardly be supported. The decision rests, rather, on two considerations, one pragmatic, the other evaluative.

The pragmatic consideration is simply this: of the 42 Christian organizations registered with the Ministry of Education as religious juridical persons as of December 31, 1988,[1] the Nihon Kirisuto Kyōdan is the one I know best and concerning which I can most readily lay my hands on the necessary data.

The evaluative consideration is that since the Nihon Kirisuto Kyōdan is far and away the largest Protestant body in Japan (139,720 members as of December 31, 1988, followed by the Matsujitsu Seito Iesu Kirisuto Kyōkai or Church of Jesus Christ of Latter-day Saints with 85,442, then the Nihon Seikōkai or Anglican Episcopal Church of Japan with 57,478), what goes on in it can hardly be ignored in any picture of Japanese Christianity.

THE TERMS "RELIGIOUS" AND "SECULAR"

Whatever else secularization may mean, it surely implies some kind of religious change in the direction of more widely secular interests. It behooves us, however, to indicate with some care what these terms will here be taken to mean.

This juxtaposing of the terms "religious" and "secular" might seem to suggest implicit or explicit acceptance of the widely used distinction between natural and supernatural, profane and sacred, empirical and transcendent. From this perspective the commonsense thing to do would be to set up a dichotomy

---

[1] *Shūkyō nenkan* [Religions yearbook] (1990), 78–81.

of realms. One would subsume the sacred, the supernatural, and the transcendent under "the religious" and the natural, the profane, and the empirical under "the secular." Then the more religious a phenomenon, the less secular it would be, and vice versa.

The difficulty with this approach is that the ontological dualism on which it depends denies by fiat the claim that what appears to be secularization can and should be understood as a revolution in religious perspectives and institutions. To accept this dualism might make for a tidy solution to the question of definition, but it would imply a deductive (if not ideological) approach to the data and rule out in advance any possibility of religious meaning in phenomena viewed through the spectacles of the secularization concept.

Even van Gennep's idea of "the pivoting of the sacred" runs into an insurmountable difficulty. His view that "sacredness as an attribute is not absolute,"[2] that it is the social stage and role that bring into play the concepts of sacred and profane, that "whoever passes through the various positions of a lifetime one day sees the sacred where before he has seen the profane, or vice versa"[3] — all this represents a distinct advance, not least because it requires researchers to use such concepts more as tools than as principles, to use them with what Ernst Troeltsch once referred to as "versatility" in the adopting of different points of view. Even this highly flexible approach, however, strictly separates the concepts of sacred and profane, religious and secular. The concept of a "secular religion" illustrates its basic difficulty. On this view the idea of a secular religion is a contradiction in terms. Yet much of the current debate over secularization hangs precisely on whether a given phenomenon is to be understood as a secularization of the religious or a sacralization of the secular. Van Gennep's dichotomy, however versatile, cannot be expected to help resolve this matter.

What is needed, then, is an approach that will permit one to

---

[2] Arnold van Gennep, *The Rites of Passage*, transl. by Monika B. Vizedom and Gabrielle L. Caffee (Chicago: University of Chicago Press, 1960), 12.

[3] van Gennep, *Rites of Passage*, 13.

treat as a possibility the idea that secularization may involve religious meaning. Selecting only a portion of the approach pioneered by Luckmann in his *The Invisible Religion*, I would like to take as my starting point this statement:

> Symbolic universes are objectivated meaning-systems that relate the experiences of everyday life to a "transcendent" layer of reality. Other systems of meaning do not point beyond the world of everyday life. . . . [4]

As applied to the ideas of "religious" and "secular," this would mean that the difference between the two could be construed as a difference in degree of comprehensiveness.[5] For present purposes, then, the following definition is offered: *a religious meaning-system is one in which everyday experiences are related to a transcendent level of reality, a secular meaning-system one in which everyday experiences are not so related.*

The question of how such a definition can accommodate the idea of a "secular religion" recurs at this point. In light of the previous discussion a secular religion may be characterized as a meaning-system that rejects religion as an appropriate self-designation while at the same time relying on assumptions and attitudes that can be understood as implying belief in or reliance on a transcendent level of reality.

No basis has been provided for arguing, however, that all secularization is bound to end up, if carried to its logical conclusion, as a secular religion. The argument is intended to support only the view that secularization may have positive religious meaning.[6] It leaves open the possibility that secularization may also entail the diminution of a religious universe of meaning. The question of how to distinguish these two consequences may be deferred for the present.

---

[4] Thomas Luckmann, *The Invisible Religion: The Problem of Religion in Modern Society* (New York: Macmillan, 1967), 44.

[5] Cf. Mary Douglas, *Implicit Meanings: Essays in Anthropology* (London: Routledge and Kegan Paul, 1975), 76.

[6] Cf. Ikado Fujio, *Sezoku shakai no shūkyō* [Religion in a secular society] (Tokyo: Nihon Kirisuto Kyōdan Shuppan Kyoku, 1972), 10–11.

SECULARIZATION THEORY

At the risk of emasculating David Martin's admirable formulation of secularization theory,[7] I should like to try the experiment of seeing how it fits, or may be modified to fit, the situation of the Nihon Kirisuto Kyōdan.

The main features of Martin's theory may be set forth in brief. First of all, he limits himself to the West and Christianity. Second, he postulates "that at certain crucial periods in their history societies acquire a particular frame and that subsequent events persistently move within the limits of that frame."[8] The crucial periods to which he has reference are the times when societies enter the modern stage, and he is particularly interested in what happens after this entrance has been made.[9] Third, he distinguishes between two types of frame, the monopolistic and the pluralistic. This feature of the theory is clarified in the following generalization: "Where there exists one religion possessed of a monopoly society splits into two warring sides, one of which is dedicated to religion. Similarly where there are two or more religions (or distinct forms of the same religion) this does not happen."[10] Fourth, he proposes a continuum ranging from total monopoly on the one hand to total laissez faire on the other, and on this continuum he locates various societies as of the time they entered modernity. Their locations he calls "categories," which he identifies as follows:

1. *Total monopoly* — where one religion exercises influence over a whole society. Essentially, this category pertains to the Catholic countries, namely, Spain and Portugal, Italy and Belgium, France and Austria.

2. *Duopoly or mixed* — Protestant societies in which Catholics constitute a large minority, such as Holland, Germany, and Switzerland.

---

[7] David Martin, *A General Theory of Secularization* (Oxford: Basil Blackwell, 1978), esp. chap. 2, "A Theory of Secularization: Basic Patterns."

[8] Martin, *Secularization*, 15. Cf. 27.

[9] Martin, *Secularization*, 13.

[10] Martin, *Secularization*, 17–18.

3. *State church*—a Protestant church-state nexus counter-balanced by various forms of religious dissent, as in England and Australia, New Zealand and Canada, and to some extent in Scandinavia.

4. *Pluralism*—the type of society in which no religious bodies have an organic link with the state, all being mutually competitive. This type is exemplified by the U.S.A.

Martin then proceeds to work out the socio-logic of these basic categories by analyzing five "universes of relationships": the Anglo-American and Scandinavian group, the Catholic group, communist regimes, the mixed group, and cultures subjected to external domination. In general terms his argument is that the more monopolistic a society at the time it enters modernity, the more social change tends toward internal violence in which religion is a major issue (unless the whole society must unite against an external threat), whereas the more pluralistic a society at the time of entry into modernity, the more social change is accommodated within a climate of political stability.

To lift up only the foregoing features, here taken as particularly germane to the present inquiry, has the virtue of economy but the vice of omitting great blocks of important and illuminating material, both empirical and analytic. Perhaps what has been presented, however, will suffice as a springboard from which to plunge into the Japanese situation.

THE FRAME

SOCIETY AND THE TRADITIONAL RELIGIONS

Japan's change from a premodern to a modern state, marked by such features as population movement to urban centers, growth of light and heavy industry, establishment of a nationwide educational system, decline in importance of kinship bonds and ties to the land, increase in bureaucratic organizations, and increase in roles based on contract and achievement,[11] is usually said to have begun with the Meiji Restoration of 1868. The restoration was occasioned by what was perceived as an external threat, namely, the "black ships" of Commodore Perry of the U.S.A. Though serious disputes occurred within Japan over whether to accede to the U.S. demand for a treaty of amity, rightly seen as a precedent for relations with other countries, and whether to maintain the shogunate or replace it with a political system governed by the emperor,[12] these disputes did not split the nation. It was united, rather, under the aegis of the emperor and the restoration government.

The place of religion in Japanese society at that time can perhaps best be understood by drawing a distinction between religious roles in relation to people in general and religious statuses relative to the government. The major institutional forms of traditional religion were Shinto and Buddhism. So far as government standing is concerned, they occupied quite different positions. The premodern government, the shogunate, had made Buddhism an agency of social control and a de facto state religion.[13] Its priests were paid by the state, and every household of commoners (farmers, craftsmen, and traders) was required not only to affiliate with a Buddhist temple but also, after 1662, to obtain annually from the priest a document certifying in effect that the possessor was a Buddhist temple supporter innocent of dangerous connections such as adherence to Christianity or other underground faiths.[14] When the restoration government took over, it simply threw out Buddhism and replaced it with Shinto. In order to purify Shinto of its Buddhist accretions, the

---

[11] Munakata Iwao, "The Ambivalent Effects of Modernization on the Traditional Folk Religion of Japan," *Japanese Journal of Religious Studies* 3 (1976): 101.

[12] Abe Yoshiya, "From Prohibition to Toleration: Japanese Government Views Regarding Christianity, 1854–73," *Japanese Journal of Religious Studies* 5 (1978): 110–11, 119.

[13] Murakami Shigeyoshi, *Nihon hyakunen no shūkyō: Haibutsu kishaku kara Sōka Gakkai made* [A hundred years of religion in Japan: From anti-Buddhist iconoclasm to Sōka Gakkai] (Tokyo: Kōdansha, 1968), 14.

[14] Kasahara Kazuo, ed. *Nihon shūkyōshi* [A history of Japanese religion] (Tokyo: Yamakawa Shuppansha, 1977), 2: 4–6. Cf. Anesaki, *History*, 260.

separation of the two was decreed,[15] and a short period of anti-Buddhist iconoclasm began. This iconoclasm terminated about 1871 when Buddhist leaders managed to have the government set up an agency for the supervision of temple affairs.[16] Shinto, however, defined as a non-religion, was established under the authority of the emperor as the state cult.[17] In line with the policy of "one shrine per village," Shinto shrines came under government scrutiny. From an original total of approximately 190,000 in 1906, the number was reduced to 127,000 by 1912.[18] These shrines, classified in various ranks, were declared places for the observance of state rites. Shinto priestly offices were made appointive rather than hereditary, but the stipends of those appointed were guaranteed by the government.

With regard to people in general, however, it is important to recognize that the notion of exclusive adherence to one religion was almost inconceivable. Most people regarded Shinto as the religion of communities and local groups, Buddhism as the religion through which they buried and venerated the dead of their households.[19] With no sense of incongruity whatever, they participated in both. Consequently, though the early Meiji years were in many ways times of tumult and turmoil, on the whole one can recognize the Japan of that time not as an internally divided society at war over the issue of religion, but as a society largely united under the authority of the emperor.

MARGINAL GROUPS

That Christianity had only a miniscule part to play, whether in the later years of the shogunate or the early years of the restora-

---

[15] Bunkachō [Agency for Cultural Affairs, Ministry of Education], *Meiji ikō shūkyō seido hyakunen shi* [Religious organizations during the hundred years since Meiji] (Tokyo: Bunkachō, 1970), 9–10.

[16] Murakami, *Nihon hyakunen no shūkyō* [A hundred years of religion in Japan], 40.

[17] Kasahara, *Nihon shūkyōshi* [A history of Japanese religion], 2: 310.

[18] Kōmoto Mitsugu, "Gendai toshi no minzoku shinkō — Kakyō saiken to chinkon" [Folk religion in the modern city: Relocating the family home and the repose of souls], in Ōmura and Nishiyama, eds., *Gendaijin no shūkyō* [The religion of present-day people], 53.

[19] Morioka Kiyomi, *Religion in Changing Japanese Society* (Tokyo: University of Tokyo Press, 1975), 6.

tion government, hardly calls for documentation. Prior to the restoration, Christianity was considered subversive of a social order in which every person had an assigned place and role and in which opportunities for social mobility were strictly limited.[20] During the first years of the Meiji government, it was regarded as a threat to the state-promulgated dogma of "theocracy" that so neatly fitted the government's "urgent need for a spiritual symbol around which to unify the new nation."[21] Not until February 24, 1873 were the notices prohibiting Christianity removed, and even then Christianity, though tolerated, remained technically illegal.

Christianity, however, was not the only illegal religious body in early Meiji Japan. Groups like Kurozumikyō, Konkōkyō, and Tenrikyō, until granted legal recognition (in 1876, 1900, and 1908 respectively), were considered illegal and subjected to severe persecution. The "legal recognition" system, moreover, was by no means incidental to the overall frame. It was a logical consequence of an assumption that guided government religious policy from 701, when the law of the land was first codified, to 1945, when World War II ended. This assumption was that religious organizations existed to serve the interests of the state. Those accorded legal recognition were rewarded with government protection and tax exemptions, but had to submit to government control and supervision. Unauthorized religious organizations were suppressed.[22]

This, then, was the "frame" established in Japan at the time that the Meiji government initiated its policy of modernization within a format of Shinto revivalism: a state ideology and cult counterbalanced by an extensive, highly proliferated, and recently disestablished Buddhism — not to mention a number of smaller, persecuted religious groups which, like Christianity, played only a minor role in the national myth.[23]

---

[20] Cf. Sugimoto and Swain, *Science and Culture*, 165, 236.

[21] Abe, "From Prohibition to Toleration," 120.

[22] Kawawata, "Religious Organizations," 162. Cf. Koike Kenji, Nishikawa Shigenori and Murakami Shigeyoshi, eds., *Shūkyō dan'atsu o kataru* [Conversations about religious persecution] (Tokyo: Iwanami Shoten, 1978).

[23] It should be mentioned that later in the same period, particularly 1882–1889,

THE NIHON KIRISUTO KYŌDAN

AMBIGUOUS ORIGIN

The Nihon Kirisuto Kyōdan came into being in June 1941 as an aggregation of some thirty-four previously autonomous Protestant denominations. Its formation was attended by both internal and external pressures. Internally, the desire for a united Protestant Christianity in Japan can be traced back to the earliest period of Japanese Protestant history.[24] From this perspective, the emergence of the Nihon Kirisuto Kyōdan in 1941 seemed providential. Externally, the pressure to unite came from the wartime Ministry of Education in accordance with its policy of establishing government control over religious organizations as part of a nationwide system of mobilization.[25] From its inception, therefore, the Nihon Kirisuto Kyōdan rested on an uneasy combination of "sacred" and "secular" motivations.

Christianity attracted a number of converts, first from the former samurai class, later from the urban white-collar class. Thus Ikado, *Sezoku shakai* [Secular society], 292–304. This was due at least in part to the fact that Christianity was regarded as a basic element in the Western civilization to which Japan looked for modernization models. Cf. Winburn T. Thomas, *Protestant Beginnings in Japan: The First Three Decades, 1859–1889* (Rutland, Vermont and Tokyo, Japan: Charles E. Tuttle, 1959), 172–3, 176. "Nation building" was thus a motivation to conversion. See Ogawa Keiji, ed., *Nihonjin to kirisutokyō* [The Japanese and Christianity] (Tokyo: Sanseidō, 1973), 268–69. During this time, Christianity may be said to have played a minor but positive role in the still growing national myth.

As a separate matter, the principle of "freedom of religious belief under the protection of the state" was communicated to religious leaders as an intrinsic part of government policy in 1875. Cf. Bunkachō, *Meiji ikō shūkyō seido* [Religious organizations since Meiji], 84; also Abe Yoshiya, "Religious Freedom under the Meiji Constitution," *Contemporary Religions in Japan* 9 (1968): 268–338. Moreover, freedom of conscience "within limits not prejudicial to peace and order, and not antagonistic to their duties as subjects" was guaranteed by the Constitution of 1889. But since Shinto (later more narrowly defined as Shrine Shinto in distinction from Sect Shinto) still functioned as the state cult even though legally characterized as a non-religious public juridical person (Kawawata, "Religious Organizations," 162–63), these alterations did not involve any basic change in the frame.

[24] Morioka Kiyomi, *Nihon no kindai shakai to kirisutokyō* [Modern Japanese society and Christianity] (Tokyo: Hyōronsha, 1970), 70–72; Ogawa, *Nihonjin to kirisutokyō* [The Japanese and Christianity], 273–76.

[25] Kuwabara Shigeo, "Nihon Kirisuto Kyōdan no naibu kokuhatsu" [Internal indictment of the United Church of Christ in Japan], *Gendai no me* 19 (1978): 89.

With the end of World War II and the freedom to remain in or leave the Nihon Kirisuto Kyōdan, some groups such as the Anglican Episcopal Church, the Japan Lutheran Church, most of the Baptist churches, etc., chose to withdraw. Even among those that chose to remain, however, one continuing source of disagreement was that of the relationship between church and state. Internal disputes having to do with this relationship, particularly during the years 1967–1970, may serve to focus the concern of this study. Three related concatenations of incidents stand out with particular prominence.

CONFESSION OF WARTIME RESPONSIBILITY

On Easter Sunday, March 26, 1967, Suzuki Masahisa, then Moderator of the Nihon Kirisuto Kyōdan, issued a statement that can be seen as the beginning of a major internal polarization.[26] It was entitled the *Dai niji taisenka ni okeru Nihon Kirisuto Kyōdan no sekinin ni tsuite no kokuhaku* ("Confession concerning the responsibility of the Nihon Kirisuto Kyōdan during World War II"). In essence it presented three points: (1) a confession that the church was mistaken to have approved of and supported the war, (2) a request for forgiveness, and (3) an expression of anxiety as to the course being taken by postwar Japan and a resolution to fulfill the role of loyal critic.

The initial debates were mild. The chief points at issue were two. First was the matter of whether the Confession struck a satisfactory balance between those who wanted to emphasize that the Nihon Kirisuto Kyōdan had been formed under government pressure and those who wanted to emphasize that its formation was an answer to prayer. Second, it was protested by some that the Confession went too far when it said that recognition of the

---

[26] The issuing of the Confession was not something the Moderator did arbitrarily. At the 14th General Assembly of the Nihon Kirisuto Kyōdan a proposal was made that the church issue a statement on its responsibility for the war. This proposal, though not passed, was referred to the Executive Committee. At its meeting on February 20–22, 1967, this committee debated the matter, revised the proposed statement, and voted 19–2 that it be issued in the form of a letter over the name of the Moderator (*Kirisutokyō nenkan* [Yearbook on Christianity] (Tokyo: Kirisuto Shinbunsha, 1968), 58).

error committed in the name of the church was "unanimous." The protestors held that this kind of acknowledgment had already been made on June 9, 1946 in a statement that former Moderator Kozaki Michio read to the National Assembly of Christians. This protest, however, merely extended the scope of the debate, for though some interpreted Kozaki's statement as a confession and asked why they were now being called on to repeat it, others viewed its remarks on error and repentance as merely incidental to its call to mission.[27]

Debates over the Confession coincided with an election for the governorship of Tokyo. Those opposed to the Confession and to Moderator Suzuki supported Matsushita Masatoshi, a Christian candidate backed by the Liberal-Democratic Party and the Social Democratic Party. The pro-Confession group supported Minobe Ryōkichi, candidate of the Socialist and Communist parties. Among the Minobe-supporters was Moderator Suzuki, acting "in an individual capacity." The division over the election intensified the drift toward polarization.

On July 6, 1967, the Executive Committee of the church appointed a special "Five-Man Committee," headed by Professor Kitamori Kazoh of Tokyo Union Theological Seminary, to deal with matters relating to the Confession. This committee, after meetings with opponents of the Confession, submitted a rather neutral report in September, but in this way the name of Professor Kitamori became definitely linked to the Confession of wartime responsibility.

EXPO

The journalistic abbreviation "Expo" refers to the Japanese International Exposition of 1970. At a general meeting of the National Christian Council on March 19, 1968, it was decided to support the idea of an ecumenical Christian pavilion at Expo. Invited to participate were the Catholic Church in Japan, the Nihon Kirisuto Kyōdan, and other churches and groups related to the National Christian Council. The cost of the pavilion was

---

[27] *Kirisutokyō nenkan* (1968), 59.

estimated at ¥100 million, of which ¥30 million was to be raised by the Catholics, ¥35 million by the Protestants, and ¥30 million through contributions from overseas.

The theme for Expo as a whole was "Human Progress and Harmony." For the Christian pavilion, it was reworded to read "Eyes and Hands—the Human Discovery," followed by the sub-theme "Harmony through Reconciliation—Progress through Creation." The chairman of the Expo Christian Pavilion Theme Committee was Professor Kitamori.

At its 15th General Assembly (October 21–24, 1968), the Nihon Kirisuto Kyōdan, after re-electing Suzuki as Moderator and Ii Kiyoshi as Vice-Moderator on the first ballot, voted to participate in the Expo Christian pavilion.[28] This decision led to further polarization.

Advocates of participation in the Christian pavilion argued that it was important for Christianity to have an opportunity to communicate the gospel to the hundreds and thousands of people expected to visit Expo. They further argued that the chance to present an ecumenical witness on such an occasion was too valuable to pass by. Opponents argued, however, that since Expo was sponsored by the government and was intended to demonstrate Japan's economic (and by implication, military) power to the world, a power derived from exploitation of people in other countries of Asia, participation in Expo would contra-dict not only the church's continuing opposition to the Yasukuni Shrine bill (a bill that would make Yasukuni Shrine a non-religious institution and support it with tax money) but also the Confession of wartime responsibility (which sought especially the forgiveness of "our brothers and sisters . . . of Asian countries").[29]

During the thick of the debates, many of which involved heated attacks on him, Moderator Suzuki fell ill. After an operation on June 9, 1969, he died of cancer of the liver on July 14, 1969. Vice-Moderator Ii automatically became the new Moderator.

About this time, another political issue came to the fore, namely, whether to support or oppose the United States–Japan

---

[28] *Kirisutokyō nenkan* (1969), 83–4.
[29] *Kirisutokyō nenkan* (1970), 61.

Security Treaty that was due for renewal in 1970. Here again the anti-Expo and anti-treaty *shakai-ha* (social activist faction) encountered the pro-Expo and pro-treaty *kyōkai-ha* (church-oriented faction). Once more political division exacerbated internal dissension.

Anti-establishment students in Christian schools, lighting on the Christian pavilion issue, made it a bone of contention not only with Christian school administrators but also with leaders of the Nihon Kirisuto Kyōdan. A delegation of students from the Theological Department of Dōshisha University, in a meeting with General Secretary Takakura Tokutarō, demanded that the action of the 15th General Assembly be rescinded. On being told that he did not possess that kind of authority, they then demanded a meeting with Moderator Ii. When he met with them, Moderator Ii accepted their petition to meet with the Standing Executive Committee and promised to hold an open session of the committee on September 1, 1969.

This special session brought together not only Moderator Ii, Secretary Kimura Tomomi, General Secretary Takakura Tokutarō, and six members of the Standing Executive Committee, but also members of the Anti-Expo Kwansei Clergy, the Struggle Committee of Kansai Gakuin Theological Department, the League of Christian Fighters from Meiji Gakuin, the Tokyo Union Theological Seminary (Student) Committee for Struggle against Expo and Yasukuni Shrine, etc.—over 150 persons in all.[30] Originally the meeting was scheduled to last from 1–5 P.M. In the event it continued until 7:30 A.M. the next morning, September 2.

Dominated by opponents of Expo participation, the meeting was conducted amid much booing and heckling. The chief arguments of the opponents were: (1) It is nonsense for the Nihon Kirisuto Kyōdan to approve the Confession of wartime responsibility and oppose the Yasukuni Shrine bill on the one hand, and on the other to participate in Expo, which has such a close connection not only with the state establishment but also with the United States–Japan Security Treaty. (2) It is absurd to

[30] *Kirisutokyō nenkan* (1970), 61.

justify participation on the ground of evangelistic witness and spend ¥100 million on a building when it is known already that there will be little evangelistic impact. (3) Cooperation with the Catholic Church is also held up as a reason for participation, but this overlooks the fact that within the Catholic Church too there is opposition to Expo participation.

During this meeting, Professor Kitamori, Chairman of the Expo Christian Pavilion Theme Committee, was slapped in the face on two occasions.

At length, the anti-Expo groups presented Moderator Ii with an ultimatum: either consider the Expo problem one of profound importance for the life of the church and convene a special General Assembly to decide the church's attitude toward it, or sever forthwith all ties with the members of the protesting groups. After a recess to confer with the Standing Executive Committee members, Moderator Ii announced that a special General Assembly would be convened either in the name of the Executive Committee or in his own name. Before it could be held, however, another series of events intervened.

TOKYO UNION THEOLOGICAL SEMINARY

After discussion at its stated meeting on September 3, 1969, the faculty of Tokyo Union Theological Seminary, the Nihon Kiri-suto Kyōdan–established school of theological education and ministerial training, issued a statement deploring the physical violence to which faculty member Professor Kitamori had been subjected. The statement called on the clergy present at the September 1 meeting, whatever their attitude toward Expo participation, to "reflect" on their failure to stop or rebuke those who struck him, thus giving tacit consent to their actions.

In response a group of Tokyo District clergy issued a statement of their own on September 6, 1969. It said that they *had* restrained those bent on violence, and it reprimanded the faculty not only for error but also for adopting an ostensibly "above the tumult" stance on the matter of Expo participation. It challenged them to make their position on Expo clear.[31]

---

[31] *Kirisutokyō nenkan* (1970), 62.

The Executive Committee of the Nihon Kirisuto Kyōdan, on September 11, 1969, held a meeting previously announced as open to committee members only. Acceding to the demand of vociferous anti-Expo auditors, however, they eventually opened it to all who wished to attend. This too turned into an all-night session. In the end, thirteen of the seventeen committee members voted to approve the convening of the special General Assembly promised by Moderator Ii. They instructed him to send out a letter to all church districts urging discussion of the Expo problem as they elected delegates to the assembly. Moderator Ii sent out such a letter on September 18, 1969.

Even earlier, though, district assemblies in certain areas had reached such a pitch of turmoil over Expo that their meetings had to be called off. The Osaka District managed to hold a special assembly on September 2–3, and at this time some 120 anti-Expo students, accepted as associate delegates, forced the Vice-Chairman of the Christian Pavilion and the Business Affairs Chief of the Christian Pavilion to tender their resignations.[32] Hyōgo District had to adjourn its meeting of May 14–15, but held another assembly on July 1, 1969, at which time the District voted to oppose Nihon Kirisuto Kyōdan participation in Expo. In the Tokyo District the Standing Committee met on September 26 with some forty anti-Expo students and pastors as auditors. This too proved to be an all-night session. It was decided to hold a special Tokyo District assembly on November 14, 1969 to air the Expo problem, and the Standing Committee was to meet again on November 7 to prepare the agenda. On that very day, however, all the officers of Tokyo District resigned, thus paralyzing further action. As it turned out, the major urban districts (Tokyo, Kanagawa, Kyoto, Osaka, and Hyōgo) found it impossible to meet to elect delegates. Nonetheless, a special General Assembly was held on November 25–26, 1969. But since anti-Expo youth, students, and clergy burst into the assembly with demands for a thorough prosecution of the Expo issue, proceedings were suspended in order to respond to their demands.

Meanwhile, at Tokyo Union Theological Seminary, leaders

---

[32] *Kirisutokyō nenkan* (1970), 63.

of the Student Self-Government Association issued a communication on September 12, 1969 calling for withdrawal of the faculty statement of September 3. It declared that until this statement was withdrawn, they would not cooperate in any way with the school. The majority of students approved this action at an assembly on September 26.[33] The student communication also called for an all-school debate, but a joint steering committee meeting scheduled for September 24 came to nothing, and one scheduled for October 1 was not held. With this, the students entered on an undeclared strike.

On November 19 the school began to receive second semester registrations (originally scheduled for October 1). But the Self-Government Association, holding that in view of the faculty statement the nature of the seminary as a whole had become questionable, declared that until clarification had been reached through general debate they would refuse to attend classes. This froze the registrations. Four student leaders, moreover, began a hunger strike to force agreement to an all-school *taishū dankō* (literally, a "mass meeting for interorganizational negotiations," but actually an assembly in which massed students would shout down all opposition and compel all but the hardiest to submit to their views). But whereas the faculty wanted to limit debate to the problem of the frozen registration process, the Self-Government Association insisted on the right to raise questions about the seminary as a whole. Neither side would budge, and from this point on, polarization proceeded apace.

On November 24, 1969, the hunger strike was called off, and the entire school was hemmed in with barricades erected by protesting students. The faculty then issued a statement saying that it would enter into no negotiations with the Self-Government Association until the barricades were removed. Thus the opposition between faculty and students that had developed since the faculty statement of September 3 became even more rigid.

Entrance examinations were scheduled for February 16, 1970. Hoping to prevent hostile students from breaking up the examinations, the faculty determined in secret to hold the

---

[33] *Kirisutokyō nenkan* (1970), 66.

examinations at over ten undisclosed locations in metropolitan and suburban Tokyo. Through information conveyed by a sympathetic professor, pro-barricade students located two of the sites and, after fighting with anti-barricade student guards, managed to force discontinuation of the examinations there. At another site, the home of a seminary professor, the pro-barricade students, frustrated by locked doors, broke a window and forced their way in. On this occasion they physically abused another professor who was present.

At this point, however, a neighbor, disturbed by the commotion, called the police. From this time on, the affair could no longer be considered intramural. Two students were indicted on suspicion of trespass.

On March 11, 1970, the seminary called in the riot police to remove the barricades. The students behind the barricades were ordered to leave, but of the eight present at that hour (6:50 A.M.), three refused and were placed under arrest. Thereupon the school surrounded the premises with an iron fence, set up a checkpoint, and notified students that registration and classes would begin on March 17. Non-registering students were invited to submit applications for leave of absence by March 31. Students who neither registered nor applied for leave of absence were warned that their names would be struck from the rolls. Some 87 students chose to register, 10 to take a leave of absence. The remainder, about one-fifth of the student body, left the seminary.

In district assemblies held throughout the nation between March and May 1970, the action taken by Tokyo Union Theological Seminary was hotly debated. The violent words and actions that characterized the all-night meeting of September 1, 1969 had counterparts in many local meetings. In the five major church districts, feelings ran so high that delegates dared not assemble for fear of outbursts of violence.[34]

Thus the rift that became evident with the announcement of the Confession of wartime responsibility widened into a gulf during the confrontations over Expo. Related actions at Tokyo

---

[34] *Kirisutokyō nenkan* (1971), 61.

Union Theological Seminary, sending shock waves throughout the church, served to make the polarization even more intense.

This sketch of events, detailed though it may seem, has omitted many developments on the one hand and stopped far short of the present on the other. But perhaps enough data are in hand to permit one to look at them from the perspective of secularization theory.

SECULARIZATION THEORY REVISITED

REFRAMING

The first point to note about what has been happening in the Nihon Kirisuto Kyōdan is that, although older people tend to predominate in the anti-Confession, pro-Expo, pro-Seminary faction and people of younger years in the pro-Confession, anti-Expo, and anti-Seminary faction, the generations are too thoroughly constitutive of both to permit one to speak with confidence of a "generation gap" that might be a consequence of different types of socialization. Yet we clearly have to do here with a *conflict of norms*. It may be advisable to begin by specifying what they are.

Those opposing the Confession, favoring participation in Expo, and supporting the action of the Seminary in calling for the riot police may be regarded as consistent adherents to the kind of norm implicit in the frame established in 1868 and perpetuated until 1945. In accordance with this frame, the government is a legitimate authority, and the church will do well to cooperate with it unless an important issue is at stake. With some tentativeness it may be suggested that people socialized in the years prior to 1945 find it easier to take this line than to question or oppose it.

On the other hand, those favoring the Confession, opposing participation in Expo, and criticizing the Seminary can be thought of as exponents of a different norm. For them the government is by no means the kind of authority whose legitimacy is to be accepted unquestioningly until an issue arises. On the contrary, they see government and big business as joined in a spiral of mounting exploitation, pollution, and dehumanization that only waits to be completed by a revival of military power and a state-inculcated ideology. In this situation the church, as they see it, must be vigilant, ready at any time to mobilize opposition to unacceptable government actions. This norm, it may be suggested, is particularly appealing to people socialized in the years following 1945.

What I am proposing, then, is that in order to understand the nature of the events that have recently taken place in the Nihon Kirisuto Kyōdan, it makes sense to postulate two coexistent frames—not for the nation as a whole, but for divided people in this church. In the first frame, government and religious organizations alike largely accept the traditional view that since religion and state are not necessarily opposed, religion should carry out its responsibilities within the framework established by the state even if this serves the interests of the state. This orientation will be referred to as the "state-over-religion" frame. In the second frame, originally imposed as a consequence of defeat in war but continued in law beyond the end of the Occupation,[35] the relationship between government and religious organizations is organized on the pattern of U.S. pluralism. No religion has an organic connection with the state. Religious teaching (and the teaching of an allegedly non-religious state ideology) is eliminated from the public school system, and the state is, in principle, neutral in its treatment of the various religious organizations. This will be referred to as the "neutral-state / pluralistic-religion" frame.

The polarization within the Nihon Kirisuto Kyōdan comes into view as a conflict between people oriented to one or the other of these two frames.[36]

RELATIONSHIPS

The issues that have brought Nihon Kirisuto Kyōdan members

---

[35] See Kawawata, "Religious Organizations," 162, 165, 168–9.

[36] Martin takes it for granted that there will be only one frame per society. I share this view at the macro level, but wish to suggest that at the micro level it is helpful to seek understanding by reference to frame conflict.

into confrontation can be treated under the headings of the relationship between Christianity and social authority on the one hand, and the relationship between Christianity and politics on the other.[37]

So far as our data show, the issue of the relationship between Christianity and politics became a matter of internal dissension in two connections: the 1967 election for governor of Tokyo, and the matter of supporting or opposing the 1970 renewal of the United States–Japan Security Treaty. In both cases the intra-church divisions took place in a way that accords with the two-frame assumption. At the time of the election, opponents of the Confession of wartime responsibility were identified as supporters of the right-wing or conservative candidate, proponents as supporters of the left-wing or progressive candidate.

Likewise with regard to the United States–Japan Security Treaty, the implication is that the former, in accordance with the position of the dominant conservative party, gave the treaty their support whereas the latter, in parallel with the progressives, opposed it. Given the percentage of Christians in Japan at that time (slightly less than 1% in 1968), this tumult within the Nihon Kirisuto Kyōdan was little more than a tempest in a teapot, for though people throughout Japan took sides on the treaty issue, their doing so did not result in a religious division. In fact one might suggest that the general practice of participating both in Shinto festivals and Buddhist household rites (quite apart from knowledge of or adherence to their teachings) contributes to a climate of political stability in that it minimizes the possibility of conflict over the issue of religion. In the Nihon Kirisuto Kyōdan, however, the fact that Christian voters took positions across the political spectrum appears to have close links with religious dissension. This may be due in part to the

---

[37] Within the church, confrontations are more likely to take place over theological issues such as Christology, biblical interpretation, the confession of faith, and the nature of the church. In focusing on the relationships with politics and social authority, I do not mean to imply that the theological discussions are mere epiphenomena. It may be suggested, however, that if the two-frame assumption helps make sense of the issues here selected for consideration, it may also throw some light on the dynamics of the theological debates.

circumstance that their religious options are at once more limited and more demanding than those of the general populace.

Under the heading of the relationship between Christianity and social authority, attention focuses on the matter of attitudes toward the legitimacy of the government, readiness to cooperate with the government, and attitudes toward the emperor system. Unfortunately, the research data known to me do not permit one to distinguish among Nihon Kirisuto Kyōdan members a tendency toward one or the other of two poles in regard to these matters. What can be said here, therefore, will of necessity be somewhat conjectural. But if the two frames are taken as ideal types, one would expect that people belonging to the state-over-religion frame would on the whole tend to accept the government as legitimate even if bound to oppose it on critical issues, to be ready and willing to cooperate with it and seek its protection, not least as a way of improving the status of Christianity, and to favor the emperor system even while hoping that it can be purified of its religious elements — or that the emperor may become a convert to Christian faith. Conversely, one would expect to find people belonging to the neutral-state / pluralistic-religion frame more ready to question the legitimacy of the government, quicker to balk at cooperating with or appealing to the government, and generally inclined to view the emperor system with disquiet if not disfavor. By the same token, whereas the neutral-state / pluralistic-religion frame would facilitate adoption of the view that the church should for religious reasons be actively engaged in sociopolitical concerns, the state-over-religion frame would require it to concentrate on preaching the gospel and building up the church.

Though an ideal type is by definition nothing but a mental construct, one would further expect that the more intense the polarization between Nihon Kirisuto Kyōdan members over such issues, the more evident an empirical approximation to these ideal types will become. By rights, these surmises should be framed as hypotheses and tested through research, but the situation within the Nihon Kirisuto Kyōdan at present makes such research unfeasible. To the extent, however, that the earlier account of events in the recent history of the Nihon Kirisuto

Kyōdan is deemed accurate, the conjectures advanced here will not seem altogether far-fetched.

So far as data now in hand are concerned, then, these two sets of relationships appear congruent with the assumption of a state-over-religion frame and a coexisting neutral-state / pluralistic-religion frame.

But if the dissension in the Nihon Kirisuto Kyōdan is understood as a conflict of norms deriving from the coexistence of frames of more general social import, it must be expected that similar conflicts have ensued or will ensue in other religious groups. Such similarity would seem most likely in groups comparable to the Nihon Kirisuto Kyōdan in respect of marginality, cultural deviance, and emphasis on individual freedom of conscience. It would be sought first, therefore, in other Protestant Christian groups, second in the Catholic Church, and, a trailing third, in some of the new religions.

WHAT IS LEFT OUT?

Even if one were to imagine, contrary to all realistic expectation, that the pluralistic frame had totally replaced the traditional frame, it would still be inconceivable that Japanese and U.S. societies could be treated as theoretically interchangeable. Secularization theory as here presented has left out, that is to say, the dimension of cultural specificity.

This point may be illustrated from three angles: language, the teacher-disciple relationship, and the permissive attitude toward violence.

That the Japanese language mirrors hierarchical concepts of social relationship is well known. One uses, for example, one class of verb endings when speaking to a superior, another when speaking to an inferior, and still a third when speaking to a friend or equal—though as Lebra has observed, the Japanese language, while rich in "status-indicative expressions," is "rather poor in status-neutral vocabulary."[38] But when so-called radical students address their professors in a *taishū dankō*, they often use

---

[38] Takie Sugiyama Lebra, *Japanese Patterns of Behavior* (Honolulu: University Press of Hawaii, 1976), 70.

coarse, rude, even insulting language. This has been described as a dramatic way of avoiding linguistic submission to the establishment.[39] The effect of such linguistic inversion has to be felt in order to be understood, but its impact in confrontations cannot be ignored.

The teacher-disciple relationship in Japan can range from mere formalism to utmost dedication, but it always represents some idea that a disciple is an "insider." Such relationships often last a lifetime and, though not without burdens, can involve great emotional satisfactions. On the other hand, the teacher-disciple relationship can also be severed. It may not be too fanciful to regard the slapping of Professor Kitamori as a symbolic rejection of his role as a teacher in the church. In this sense it can be viewed as a "licensed and expected" contravention of an ideal normative system.[40] That the slapping was a form of hostility hardly need be argued. The point is, rather, that in the Japanese cultural context the coarse language and physical contact can be seen as a message conveyed through symbolic inversion of a relationship that would ordinarily have called for deferential language and physical distance.

The violence directed toward Professor Kitamori, the physical abuse of another seminary professor, the use of sticks and clubs not only to threaten but also to injure and draw blood[41] — such acts are not without precedent elsewhere, but a cultural element appears to come into play as regards the ease with which such behavior is excused in Japan. The basis on which it is excused is not the principle that in certain situations violence can be tolerated. It is the view that purity of heart on the part of the relatively powerless perpetrator excuses his or her violence. This, together with a ready sympathy for those whose ideas are ignored in the shaping of a consensus,[42] gives a certain culturally

---

[39] Higa Masamori as cited in Lebra, *Patterns*, 71–2.

[40] Roger D. Abrahams and Richard Bauman, "Ranges of Festival Behavior," in Barbara A. Babcock, ed., *The Reversible World: Symbolic Inversion in Art and Society* (Ithaca: Cornell University Press, 1978), 196.

[41] *Kirisutokyō nenkan* [Yearbook on Christianity] (1972), 68.

[42] Cf. Edwin O. Reischauer, *The Japanese* (Cambridge, Massachusetts: Belknap Press of Harvard University Press, 1977), 188.

supported expectation of impunity to those who choose to employ violence.

In these and other ways, then, cultural elements play an important and irreducible role in the process of religious change seen in the Nihon Kirisuto Kyōdan. The problem to be noted here is not that such elements cannot be woven into the theory, but that the theory provides no criteria whereby to assess the weight to be attached to such elements.

AN UNANSWERED QUESTION

The question deferred for later consideration was that of how to determine whether secularization represents a decline or a re-orientation of religious interests. With specific reference to the Nihon Kirisuto Kyōdan and the events of 1967–1970, which assessment, if either, is to be made?

One way of answering this question might be to ask the principals. This, however, would be inconclusive because, whereas some people insist that the anti-Expo "radicals" are self-lessly devoted to working out in society the implications of Christian discipleship (not necessarily churchmanship), others contend that their views on Christ and the church are heretical and will lead to the mongrelization of Christian faith, and still others are simply too confused or apathetic to answer the question.

Another way might be to answer the question in terms of criteria proposed by the inquirer. This, however, would be equally inconclusive because the assessment as to decline or reorientation would vary from person to person in accordance with each one's conception of history and religion. In the words of Glock and Stark, "Ideological commitments to different conceptions of what it means to be religious cannot be resolved scientifically."[43]

For the present, therefore, this question is unanswerable and

---

[43] Charles Y. Glock and Rodney Stark, *Religion and Society in Tension* (Chicago: Rand McNally, 1965), 85. Cf. Richard K. Fenn, "The Secularization of Values: An Analytical Framework for the Study of Secularization," *Journal for the Scientific Study of Religion* 8 (1969): 114.

must remain so until we learn to take account of the problem of metatheoretical assumptions to which Luckmann has directed us.[44]

CONCLUSION

The focal question of this inquiry has been whether the secularization theory proposed by Martin can help make intelligible what has been happening in recent years in the Nihon Kirisuto Kyōdan. In my judgment this question can be answered in the affirmative if the theory is modified to accommodate the idea of two coexistent frames.[45]

This judgment rests primarily on the evident coherence between the theoretical structure and the data. It would be more secure, I believe, had it been possible to show that the more factors a, b, and c come into play, the more a trend toward x, y, and z can be seen among Nihon Kirisuto Kyōdan members. Unfortunately, neither theory nor methodology presently permit that kind of demonstration. Nonetheless, this application of secularization theory has, I believe, thrown some light on the problems that have divided Nihon Kirisuto Kyōdan members for the last two decades.

---

[44] Thomas Luckmann, "Theories of Religion and Social Change," *Annual Review of the Social Sciences of Religion* 1 (1977): 1–27.

[45] Whether this theory can help make intelligible the developments in Japanese religion and society as a whole is quite another question. One of the main problems of determining its applicability on a larger scale would be that of transplanting it from a cultural context where religious adherence is exclusive to one where it is not. Since one could still determine a frame (or frames) and analyze relationships, however, this problem would not seem insurmountable.

For a discussion of secularization in relation to Japanese religion and society as a whole, see Jan Swyngedouw ("Secularization in a Japanese Context," *Japanese Journal of Religious Studies* 3 (1976): 283–306 and "Japanese Religiosity in an Age of Internationalization," *Japanese Journal of Religious Studies* 5 (1978): 87–106). For an argument supporting the view that the concept of secularization as a crisis in institutional religion is not applicable to Japanese society as a whole, see Yanagawa Keiichi and Abe Yoshiya, "Some Observations on the Sociology of Religion in Japan," *Japanese Journal of Religious Studies* 5 (1978): 5–27, "Reply," *Japanese Journal of Religious Studies* 5 (1978): 33–36, and "Cross-cultural Implications." For opposing views, see Jan Swyngedouw, "A Rejoinder," *Japanese Journal of Religious Studies* 5 (1978): 28–32 and David Reid, "Reflections: A Response to Professors Yanagawa and Abe," *Japanese Journal of Religious Studies* 10 (1983): 309–15.

Chapter 5

Remembering the Dead

THE QUESTION TO BE EXAMINED here is whether there is presumptive evidence that Protestant Christianity in Japan has been influenced by the ancestral rite tradition in such a way that one must take this influence into account in order to understand contemporary Japanese Protestantism.[1]

That Japanese culture includes a deep-rooted ancestral cult tradition has long been established.[2] It is equally well established

---

[1] Japanese terms denoting post-funeral mortuary rites include *ireisai* 慰霊祭 (a Shinto ritual to comfort and console the spirits), *senzo kuyō* 先祖供養 (a Buddhist ritual at which people offer prayers for the repose of one or more ancestors), *sosen sūkei* 祖先崇敬 (to offer homage or respect to ancestors), *sosen saishi* 祖先祭祀 (ancestral rites), etc. Probably the most generally used term is *sosen sūhai* 祖先崇拝 . To translate this term as "ancestor worship," though linguistically correct, sometimes leads to misunderstanding because of the theological overtones that accompany current usage of the English word "worship" in cultures largely informed by the Judeo-Christian tradition. In order to avoid such overtones — and because the Japanese term is in any case merely a translation of a Western term — I propose to use terms such as "ancestral cult," "ancestral rites," "ancestor veneration," "remembering the dead," etc. Cf. Takeda Chōshū, "Sosen sūhai (Nihon)" [Ancestor worship (Japan)], in Oguchi and Hori, eds., *Shūkyōgaku jiten* [Dictionary of religious studies], 514–16; David L. Doerner, "Comparative Analysis of Life after Death: Folk Shinto and Christianity," *Japanese Journal of Religious Studies* 4 (1977): 164; Clark Offner, "Continuing Concern for the Departed," *Japanese Religions* 11 (1979): 1–6; Shibata Chizuo, "Christianity and Japanese Ancestor Worship Considered as a Basic Cultural Form," *Northeast Asia Journal of Theology*, nos. 22–23 (1979): 62–71.

[2] Basic references include: Yanagita Kunio, "Senzo no hanashi" [The story of our ancestors], in *Teihon Yanagita Kunio shū* [Definitive edition of the collected works of Yanagita Kunio] (Tokyo: Iwanami Shoten, 1962), 10: 1–152; Aruga Kizaemon, "Kazoku no kokusai hikaku" [An international comparison of the family], in *Aruga Kizaemon chosaku shū* [Collected works of Aruga Kizaemon] (Tokyo: Miraisha, 1970),

that Buddhism, on reaching Japan, underwent considerable modification because of its accommodation to this tradition.[3] The question arises, therefore, whether Japanese Christianity, like Christianity in other parts of the world, also shows evidence of change attributable to the ancestral rite tradition.[4]

To date, surprisingly little research has been done on this question. Studies dealing with Japanese Catholics tend to focus on the *kakure kirishitan*, or "hidden Christians," though there is one study of a contemporary Catholic parish in Yokohama.[5] Studies on the "indigenization" of Japanese Protestantism tend to focus on the question of how this form of Christianity has influenced Japanese society.[6] Only rarely is the converse question posed.[7] This is largely unexplored territory.

9:174–78; Hozumi Nobushige, *Ancestor-Worship and Japanese Law*, 2nd and rev. ed. (Tokyo: Maruzen, 1912); Herman Ooms, "The Religion of the Household: A Case Study of Ancestor Worship in Japan," *Contemporary Religions in Japan* 8 (1967): 201–333 and "A Structural Analysis of Japanese Ancestral Rites and Beliefs," in William H. Newell, ed., *Ancestors* (The Hague: Mouton, 1976); Fujii Masao, *Gendaijin no shinkō kōzō* [The faith-structure of modern Japanese people] (Tokyo: Hyōronsha, 1974); William H. Newell, "Good and Bad Ancestors," in Newell, ed., *Ancestors* (The Hague: Mouton, 1976); David Plath, "Where the Family of God is the Family: The Role of the Dead in Japanese Households," *American Anthropologist* 66 (1964): 300–17; Robert J. Smith, *Ancestor Worship in Contemporary Japan* (Stanford, California: Stanford University Press, 1974) and "Who are the 'Ancestors' in Japan? A 1963 Census of Memorial Tablets," in Newell, ed., *Ancestors* (1976); Takeda Chōshū, *Sosen sūhai — Minzoku to rekishi* [Ancestor worship: Ethnology and history] (Kyoto: Heirakuji Shoten, 1957) and "Sosen sūhai (Nihon)" [Ancestor worship (Japan)], in Oguchi and Hori, eds., *Shūkyōgaku jiten* [Dictionary of religious studies], 514–16; Tanaka Hisao, *Sosen saishi no kenkyū* [Ancestral rite studies] (Tokyo: Kōbundō, 1978).

[3] Watanabe Shōkō, *Nihon no bukkyō* [Japanese Buddhism] (Tokyo: Iwanami Shoten, 1958), 102–20; Takeda, *Sosen sūhai* [Ancestor worship], 214–44; Nakamura Hajime, *Ways of Thinking of Eastern Peoples*, 424–25.

[4] For the influence of ancestral rites on Christianity in Africa, see Bronislaw Malinowski, *The Dynamics of Culture Change* (New Haven: Yale University Press, 1945). For a study of changing funeral customs in Japan, see Nakamaki Hirochika, "Continuity and Change: Funeral Customs in Modern Japan," *Japanese Journal of Religious Studies* 13 (1986): 177–92.

[5] On the *kakure kirishitan*, see Furuno Kiyoto, *Kakure kirishitan* [Underground Christians] (Tokyo: Shibundō, 1959) and "Kirishitanizumu no hikaku kenkyū" [A comparative study of Christian syncretism], in *Furuno Kiyoto chosaku shū* [Collected works of Furuno Kiyoto] (Tokyo: San'itsu Shobō, 1973), vol. 5. On the Catholic parish in Yokohama, see Doerner, "Comparative Analysis."

[6] As in Morioka, *Nihon no kindai shakai to kirisutokyō* [Modern Japanese society and Christianity], 251–83.

[7] See Morioka Kiyomi, "Nihon nōson ni okeru kirisutokyō no juyō" [Reception

METHOD

To speak of "influence" from the ancestral rite tradition implies that Japanese Protestantism today differs from the Protestantism that arrived in Japan with the first missionaries. But any attempt to demonstrate difference runs into the difficulty that the earlier form can no longer be adequately recovered.[8] This means that we must make do with a baseline depiction that, though not without empirical warrant, is to some extent conjectural.

Before attempting this baseline depiction, however, I propose to begin by describing Japanese mortuary rites as generally practiced today—and presumably, except for minor changes, a century ago as well. The description will be analytic, the terms of analysis being drawn from the theories of Hertz and van Gennep. This should give us some idea as to what kind of change, if any, to look for in Japanese Protestantism.

THEORETICAL ORIENTATION

Robert Hertz, in his 1907 essay "The Collective Representation of Death," focuses on the phenomenon of "double burial." He finds particularly important the intermediate period between provisional and final disposal of the corpse. For this period he demonstrates that there is "a kind of symmetry or parallelism between the condition of the body . . . and the condition of the soul."[9] This symmetry is such that the soul can be ritually incorporated into the world of the dead only when society, with the end of the mourning period, will have completed its action on the body. The deceased's integration into the world of the dead is correlated, then, with the survivors' reintegration into the world of the living. Both forms of integration terminate a stage of liminality, a stage Hertz deems more important for understanding the values and institutions of the living than either the provisional or final ceremonies.

---

of Christianity in a Japanese rural community], in *Kindai shisō no keisei* [The development of modern thought], rev. ed. (Tokyo: Ochanomizu Shobō, 1959), 193–240.

[8] Cf. Malinowski, *Dynamics*, chap. 3.

[9] Robert Hertz, "A Contribution to the Study of the Collective Representation of Death," in *Death and the Right Hand*, transl. by Rodney and Claudia Needham (Glencoe, Illinois: The Free Press, 1960), 45.

Arnold van Gennep, drawing in part on Hertz's analysis, introduces his now classic book on rites of passage by classifying them into "rites of separation, transition rites, and rites of incorporation."[10] When he considers death and mortuary rites, he observes:

> On first considering funeral ceremonies, one expects rites of separation to be their most prominent component, in contrast to rites of transition and rites of incorporation. . . . A study of the data, however, reveals that the rites of separation are few in number and very simple, while the transition rites have a duration and complexity sometimes so great that they must be granted a sort of autonomy.[11]

With this statement van Gennep, like Hertz, directs our attention to the stage of liminality. His point is that after the initial rites of separation, the deceased and his or her surviving kin, especially close kin, constitute a group that exists in a marginal state between the world of the living and the world of the dead. They remain in that state until the deceased is incorporated into the one and the survivors are reincorporated into the other — generally at the end of a ritual process that varies in length and complexity from culture to culture.

A METHODOLOGICAL REFINEMENT

Against this background, we turn now to an analytical description of Japanese mortuary rites as generally practiced today. To guide this part of the inquiry, we begin with the question: How does one become an "ancestor" in a Japanese household?

This form of the question, however, is deceptively simple. It assumes that the term "ancestor" is a monovalent category — a dubious assumption.[12] In its broadest sense the term *sosen* or "ancestor" applies to all the household dead, all who have "gone before," even if they are children of living people. Analytically, however, scholars distinguish between two main classes: the

---

[10] van Gennep, *Rites of Passage*, 11 (italics omitted).
[11] van Gennep, *Rites of Passage*, 146.
[12] Cf. Lebra, *Patterns*, 222, 228.

founding ancestor or *senzo*, and the subsequent body of ancestors or *sosen*. The second class embraces the long-departed dead, the recently dead, and those who die "abnormally," that is, in infancy, childhood, or an unmarried state. Strictly speaking, the form of the question that should be considered here is: how does one who has died recently and normally come to be regarded either as the founding ancestor of a household or as one with the household body of ancestors? As a matter of convenience, however, I propose to consider only the latter half of this question. How does one who has died recently and normally become integrated into the household body of ancestors?[13]

THE JAPANESE *IE*

To review what has been written about the Japanese *ie*, or household, as a systemic entity is not necessary here. It will suffice to say that the *ie* system, understood as a corporate unit of main and branch households that share ritual obligations to their ancestors and supportive obligations to each other, is generally regarded as the key social institution that undergirds and requires the ancestral cult.

This system, relatively stable during the Edo period when social classes were largely fixed and population movement largely prohibited, has become increasingly unstable since the Meiji period.[14] In the Meiji period, the social classes of feudalism

---

[13] This inquiry will not, therefore, consider the ritual enshrinement of soldiers who die while serving "emperor and country," the relationship of the household ancestors to the imperial ancestors, the subject of fictitious ancestors, the problem of suicide, or the problem of *muenbotoke* (people who die with no kin to remember them, or whose line dies out) and how living people guard against that fearful prospect. This limitation rules out consideration not only of Shinto mortuary rites but also of locally distinctive practices such as the dual grave system in Wakayama (Tanaka, *Sosen saishi* [Ancestral rite], i, iii, vii) and the exhumation and washing of bones in Okinawa (Clarence J. Glacken, *The Great Loochoo: A Study of Okinawan Village Life* (Berkeley and Los Angeles: University of California Press, 1955; Rutland, Vermont and Tokyo, Japan: Charles E. Tuttle, 1960), 248; William P. Lebra, *Okinawan Religion: Belief, Ritual, and Social Structure* (Honolulu: University of Hawaii Press, 1966), 200–201). The focus is on "normal" death and its rituals, which in form are mainly Buddhist (Bukkyō Bunka Kenkyūkai, ed., *Senzo kuyō* [Services for the repose of the ancestors] (Osaka: Hikari no Kuni, 1977), 40–41).

[14] Cf. Hozumi, *Ancestor-Worship*, 114, 178; Tamaki Hajime, "Nihon no kazoku:

were abolished, military conscription took great numbers of young men out of fixed familiar surroundings, and population mobility and urbanization increased. These changes were only partly counterbalanced by a legal system that gave a household head (usually an eldest son) complete rights over the household property and near-absolute authority over the household members, and by an educational system that took the *ie* system as a social fundament and added to it the ideology of the family-state governed in the name of an absolute emperor and his ancestors.

Since 1945, the educational system has dropped the absolute-emperor/family-state ideology. The legal system has for the most part adopted the principle of equal property rights among all legitimate heirs.[15] The proportion of the population engaged in agriculture, fishing, and the like has dwindled from about one-half to less than one-fifth. Until very recently people have been moving in large numbers into big cities for employment, living as de facto nuclear families in small apartments with neither kami altar nor buddha altar where ancestral rites might be performed—and with no grandparents to set an example for grandchildren. As a result, this basic social institution on which the ancestral cult rests, though by no means moribund, has become decreasingly influential. Nonetheless, it remains a force to be reckoned with, not least because it functions as a prototype to which Japanese people seem to turn almost instinctively when they develop a social organization.[16] It is primarily in relation to this institutional system that the question is raised as to how one who has died recently and normally comes to be incorporated into the body of ancestors.

Seido to jittai no rekishi" [The Japanese family: A history of its structure and actual condition], *Jurisuto*, no. 6 (1977): 30–40.

[15] This principle is compromised to some extent by a Civil Code provision (Art. 897) which says: "The right to ownership of the family genealogy, ritual paraphernalia, and tomb . . . shall be inherited, in accordance with the customs of society, by the person responsible for observance of the rites for ancestors." Japanese text in Takeda Chōshū, *Nihonjin no "ie" to shūkyō* [The Japanese "household" and religion], 189 (my translation).

[16] See Morioka Kiyomi, *Shinshū kyōdan to "ie" seido* [The Shinshū Buddhist orders and the *ie* system] (Tokyo: Sōbunsha, 1962).

MORTUARY RITES

Hertz, it will be recalled, sought to explicate the phenomenon of the double burial, mainly among the Dayaks of Borneo. It may seem surprising to apply the double burial idea to Japan, but I think I can show that there is good reason to do so. What follows is a brief, ideal-type description of the Japanese funeral and post-funeral rites, analyzed in accordance with van Gennep's three ritual stages: separation, transition, and incorporation.

The rites performed between death and cremation correspond to what van Gennep calls "rites of separation."[17] Here one finds the first of the actions on the body, such as giving the dead person a last drop of water (*shini mizu*); washing the corpse, plugging all orifices, closing its eyes, and covering its face; laying it out head north and face west, dressed in white as if for pilgrimage (though black is increasingly common); and providing it with a bladed weapon as well as with food and drink. Actions that can be considered as part of the "setting of the stage" include closing the kami altar; choosing the funeral day (being sure to avoid the day called *tomobiki*, "a friend will follow"); contacting those who should be quickly informed and sending out other messages and announcements; arranging for the black-banded photograph, flowers, fruit, and other paraphernalia used at the wake and funeral (both of which usually take place in the home); and requesting a priest to chant the "pillow sutra," provide a posthumous Buddhist name on a temporary mortuary tablet, and officiate at the services. At the funeral proper, after the sutra chanting, considerable time is allotted to representatives of groups with whom the deceased was associated so that they may eulogize him or her, often in direct address. Viewing of the body, if allowed at all, takes place through a window in the coffin that exposes only the face. In an apparent attempt to minimize the pollution of death by using a "throwaway" item,

---

[17] Information on the rites between death and cremation is drawn primarily from the Bukkyō Bunka Kenkyūkai, ed., *Butsuji no shikitari* [Proper behavior at Buddhist ceremonies] (Osaka: Hikari no Kuni, 1976), from its *Senzo kuyō* [Services for the repose of the ancestors], and from Inokuchi Shōji, *Nihon no sōshiki* [The Japanese funeral] (Tokyo: Chikuma Shobō, 1977).

the coffin is nailed shut not with a hammer but with a stone, immediate family members and close kin each delivering a symbolic rap or two—often a heartrending act of separation. During the procession to the hearse and crematorium, if the deceased was the head of the house, the mortuary tablet, inscribed with the posthumous name, is carried by his or her successor—a symbolic act of considerable importance.[18] Relatives carry the coffin to the house entrance, non-relatives to the hearse and into the crematorium. At the crematorium the priest chants a sutra as the coffin and corpse are consumed by the flames. When the cremation is finished, an attendant brings the ashes on a tray to a table. As the priest chants another sutra, the attendant, using chopsticks, picks out special pieces, such as the Adam's apple (*shari* or *nodobotoke*), which the person in charge of the mortuary tablet receives with another pair of chopsticks and places into a special urn. (At no other time is it proper to transfer anything from one set of chopsticks directly to another.) The urn is then wrapped in white, carried by the tablet-bearer to the home, and formally installed, along with the mortuary tablet, in the buddha altar. In Hertz's terms, this is the first, provisional "burial." The rites from death to cremation take a comparatively short time—usually two, sometimes three, days.

Van Gennep's liminal stage, the one marked by "rites of transition," may usefully be thought of as applying in different ways to the living members and recently deceased member of the household. For both, the period between cremation and the forty-ninth day is clearly demarcated; for both, this period is followed by another, less restrictive period; but whereas this period following the forty-ninth day lasts about one year for the living, it lasts about thirty-three years for the dead.

So far as the living are concerned, the period between cremation and the forty-ninth day, the time when the pollution of death is strongest, may be called one of "primary mourning." The obligations and taboos of this period fall most heavily on the surviving spouse and successor, less heavily on other family

---

[18] Cf. Yonemura Shōji, "*Dōzoku* and Ancestor Worship in Japan," in Newell, ed., *Ancestors*, 178.

members and immediate kin. These obligations and taboos include the wearing of somber clothing, avoidance of meat, non-participation in public entertainments, and avoidance of the Shinto shrine and its festivals. This is also the time when messages of appreciation are sent to those who attended the wake or funeral, together with a gift in return for each money-gift received (or an announcement that all money-gifts are being turned over to an appropriate charity). If there is no family grave, this is the time to lease a lot and have a stone cut and ritually installed. The priest is called on to officiate at two rituals during this period: one on the seventh, the other on the forty-ninth day after death. At the conclusion of the forty-ninth day ritual, two "permanent" mortuary tablets are prepared: one for the Buddhist temple and one for the house. The urn of ashes is generally placed in the grave at this time. This corresponds to what Hertz calls the "final burial."

For the living, the forty-ninth day marks the lifting of mourning restrictions and a return to normal life. The "rite of reincorporation" is usually a meal. In fact, however, the deceased's spouse and/or successor, and sometimes the immediate family, continue to observe a few restrictions for approximately one year. For example, there will be no exchange of felicitations during the first New Year after the death,[19] and any prospective marriage or remarriage is usually postponed. This period, from the forty-ninth day to the first anniversary of the death, may be identified as one of "secondary mourning."

For the dead, this final burial can be seen as a "rite of incorporation" whereby the deceased is integrated into the realm of departed spirits. This does not mean, however, that he or she is now an "ancestor." There is more "ritual work" to be done.

After the forty-ninth day, two sets of rituals come into play, one linear, the other cyclical. The linear series has its center in

---

[19] The family customarily mails a printed postcard to people and institutions likely to send New Year's greetings, informing them of the death. The implicit message is: "We will not be sending New Year greetings next time. Please do not send us any." In this case even oral New Year's greetings are avoided because of the sense of congratulation they imply.

the *hōji* rites. These are held at the Buddhist temple, with a priest as officiant, on the first anniversary of the death and on or near the anniversaries of subsequent years that include two numbers traditionally valued in Buddhism, namely, three and seven (thus years 3, 7, 13, 17, 23, 27, and 33).[20] On or near the death anniversaries of the intervening years are the *meinichi* rites. These are generally held in the home before the buddha altar. The appropriate mortuary tablet is placed in a central position, and incense is burned and prayers offered for his or her repose. Both the *hōji* and the *meinichi* rites, with the passage of time, tend to become pleasant family reunions.

The cyclical rites are likewise of two kinds. On the one hand are the times when family members (or one representing all) visit the household grave. These times, called *higan*, embrace the spring and fall equinoxes. They are times for cleaning the gravesite, pruning its shrubbery, burning incense, and offering prayer. The brief rite is often followed by a picnic lunch. On the other hand are the times when the spirits of the dead visit the family. This takes place at midsummer during a four- or five-day period called *bon*. It is marked by such rites as the building of a welcoming fire (*mukaebi*), the erection of a temporary altar (*shōryōdana*) for the mortuary tablets and for gifts of fruit and vegetables, and a fire to see the spirits off (*okuribi* or, if lighted candles are floated away on water, a *tōrō nagashi*).[21] This too is commonly a time for visiting the household grave.

During this thirty-three year period, the deceased has an individual mortuary tablet. It is kept in the household buddha altar (with a duplicate in the temple) and is central to the services held in honor of the person it represents. At the end of this period, it is either turned over to the temple or, after a brief service, burned. Individual identity disappears. The deceased

---

[20] Why end with 33? Actually, some go on to 50 or even 100. Whatever the final year, the common explanation is that by this time the deceased no longer lives in the memories of the living. From this point of view, the precise terminal number is unimportant. But insofar as 33 is used, it may have some connection, presently obscure, with the myth of Buddha's descent to earth from Trāyastriṃśā, the heaven of the thirty-three.

[21] Inokuchi, *Nihon no sōshiki* [The Japanese funeral], 67–9, 128, 205–15.

blends into "the body of ancestors." This is the final ritual of incorporation.

In sum, the liminal process for close living survivors entails a forty-nine day period of major rituals and taboos followed by partial reincorporation into the mundane world and a one-year period of minor rituals and taboos followed by complete reincorporation. For the deceased the liminal process entails the same forty-nine day period of major rituals followed by partial incorporation into the ranks of the dead, then a thirty-three year period of linear and cyclical rites followed by complete incorporation into the status of "ancestor." Among these rites of separation, transition, and incorporation, the liminal rites occupy a place of special importance. If it is theoretically permissible to distinguish "separation-rite cultures," "liminal-rite cultures," and "incorporation-rite cultures," Japan can be regarded as belonging to the cultures that emphasize liminal rites.

WESTERN PROTESTANTISM AND INSTANT DEATH

Protestant Christianity's first significant contact with Japanese culture can usefully be dated from 1859–1860 when Episcopalian, Presbyterian, Reformed, and Baptist missionaries arrived from the United States. In order to establish some kind of baseline from which change can be recognized, I shall make two suppositions: (1) that the early Japanese converts took as normative what they were taught by the first missionaries, and (2) that these missionaries in turn took for granted that the funeral rites and associated beliefs generally held in the United States as of the mid-nineteenth century were normative for the new churches.

Unfortunately, no detailed studies of deathways in the United States have yet become available,[22] but one point suggests itself as worthy of note. It comes from France, but appears applicable to the United States as well. Robert Hertz writes:

In our own society the generally accepted opinion is that death occurs in one instant. The only purpose of the two or

---

[22] Cf. Richard Huntington and Peter Metcalf, *Celebrations of Death: The Anthropology of Mortuary Ritual* (Cambridge: Cambridge University Press, 1979), 186, 200–201.

three days' delay between the demise and the burial is to allow material preparations to be made and to summon relatives and friends. No interval separates the life ahead from the one that has just ceased: no sooner has the last breath been exhaled than the soul appears before its judge and prepares to reap the reward for its good deeds or to expiate its sins.[23]

Actually, Hertz makes it a little easy for himself here. The idea of immediate translation into the next world finds support in the words attributed to Jesus: "Today you will be with me in paradise" (Lk. 23:43). The New Testament also holds, however, that the dead are "asleep" and will be resurrected on the last day (I Cor. 15:2–22). In this case incorporation into the next world is postponed. But in neither case is it necessary for the living to perform post-funeral rites in order to assure the dead that they are remembered or to effect their incorporation into the next world. In this sense Hertz is right when he says that "death occurs in one instant."

The Protestant Christians of the United States in the mid-nineteenth century, if not now, can be classified as belonging to a culture that emphasizes separation rites almost to the exclusion of rites of transition and incorporation. The dead, moreover, come from the nuclear family—linked to other families patrilineally, matrilineally, and affinally, to be sure, but not as an entity that tends to give rise to a corporation of households singly and jointly responsible to perform rituals on behalf of their ancestors.

METHODOLOGICALLY SUGGESTIVE CONTRASTS

The nineteenth century contact between Protestant Christianity and the Japanese ancestral cult took place, then, against the background of cultures that contrasted in two respects germane to this inquiry. The U.S. bearers of the new religion came from a culture that gave primacy to the nuclear family and to short-term separation rites for the family dead. The Japanese receivers

---

[23] Hertz, "Contribution," 28.

of the new religion came from a culture that gave primacy to the *ie* system and to long-term liminal rites for the household dead.

These contrasts, in turn, give us some idea of where to look for changes in Protestant Christianity that may have resulted from contact with the Japanese ancestral cult tradition. They suggest that if such changes exist, we should expect to find them in relation to the *ie* system on the one hand, and in relation to the liminal rite custom on the other.

THE FIRST GENERATION

From the supposition that the first Protestant missionaries took the mortuary customs of their native culture as normative for the new churches, it follows that they would have taught Japanese converts to abjure what they perceived as "idol worship." And from the supposition that the early Japanese converts took the teaching of the missionaries as normative, it follows that converts must have come into serious conflict with other people, sometimes in their own household and wider circle of linked households, sometimes in their communities, sometimes in relation to the national government.[24] On the evidence available, both inferences seem warranted.

Perhaps the most famous example of a Japanese Protestant who took the "idol worship" position seriously is Niijima Jō. Niijima smuggled himself out of Japan and went to the U.S. in 1864, returned in 1874, and in 1875 founded what is now Dōshisha University. Ordained in Boston in 1873, Niijima, on returning to Japan, visited his parents in Annaka and found them offering thanks for his safe return before the kami altar. "Explaining that it was wrong for human beings to worship as God things made of wood and stone, I promptly removed the kami altar, took it into the garden, and burned it."[25]

Before leaving Annaka, he also wrote, at the request of an inquirer, an introduction to Christian faith in which he laid down two rules:

---

[24] See Abe, "From Prohibition to Toleration."

[25] Cited in Morioka, *Nihon no kindai shakai to kirisutokyō* [Modern Japanese society and Christianity], 106. My translation.

> Believing with all your heart that in heaven and earth
> there is but one true God and that beside him the kami and
> buddhas are nothing, respect him, worship him, and pray to
> him. It is the duty of descendants to respect their ancestors
> and uphold their honor, but to worship them or make them
> objects of devotion is wrong.[26]

Niijima held fast to these principles all his life.

The first generation of Protestant Christians was enjoined
to follow the position for which Niijima had become a spokes-
man.[27] Many disposed of their family's kami and buddha altars,
either burning them or storing them in an outbuilding.[28] They
refused to participate in Shinto or Buddhist rituals of any kind,
knowing that taking this stand meant that except for family
members who became Christian, they could not attend the
funerals of their parents, brothers, or sisters. The general horror
and revulsion this attitude and iconoclasm inspired can only be
imagined.

This is not to say that Christianity was regarded as totally
opposed to what was valued in the new Japan. On the contrary,
it enjoyed a certain prestige because of its association with the
scientifically and technologically advanced West. Its Christmas,
first celebrated as a Japanese church festival in 1874—complete
with tree, carols, and Santa Claus—won immediate popularity.
Its representatives put into practice a number of ideas that took
root, ideas such as education for women, abolition of concubi-
nage and legal prostitution, and to some extent even temperance.
For a brief time Japanese Christians enjoyed the experience of
being regarded as significant participants in the building of the
new nation.

---

[26] Cited in Morioka, *Nihon no kindai shakai to kirisutokyō* [Modern Japanese society
and Christianity], 106. My translation.

[27] Otis Cary, *A History of Christianity in Japan: Roman Catholic, Greek Orthodox, and
Protestant Missions* (Rutland, Vermont and Tokyo, Japan: Charles E. Tuttle, 1976), 2:
145, 161–62, 198.

[28] Morioka, *Nihon no kindai shakai to kirisutokyō* [Modern Japanese society and Chris-
tianity], 107. Note, however, that Protestants who retained the buddha altar and mortuary tablets appear to have found it impossible *not* to participate in Buddhist rites for
the departed on the anniversaries of their deaths and at the time of *bon*. See Morioka,
Nihon no kindai shakai to kirisutokyō, 141–42.

Protestant refusal to participate in the mortuary rites of other religions did not, however, insulate the Protestants against influence from mortuary rite customs divorced from their "original" religious matrix. The first Protestant funeral for which a sketchy description is available took place in March 1887.[29] Professor Morioka describes it:

> The funeral was held at the deceased's home with the pastor as officiant and with members of the church participating in Bible reading and the singing of hymns. But going in and out from the kitchen, members of the linked households and of the neighborhood work crews dug the grave and made other arrangements in the way they had always done. In addition rites were held every seven days beginning with the seventh day and ending on the forty-ninth. Rites were also held on the death anniversaries and at the *bon* season, no longer in connection with the Buddhist temple or priest but in accordance with the customs generally practiced in a provincial district heavily influenced by the relationship with priest and temple.[30]

To what extent this practice of post-separation rites was general among Japanese Protestants cannot be determined, but Morioka's description gives clear indication of early influence from the ancestral cult tradition, particularly in the protraction of mortuary rites.

THE SECOND GENERATION

After about 1890, Japanese Protestantism seems to have taken on a somewhat different character. Its members no longer laid iconoclastic hands on the household altars,[31] and some doubtless participated in the mortuary rites of other religions—not to mention the national rites of the "non-religion," State Shinto.

---

[29] Until 1884 Christian funerals were illegal. Only Shinto and Buddhist priests could perform funerals.

[30] Morioka, *Nihon no kindai shakai to kirisutokyō*, 142. My translation.

[31] Morioka, *Nihon no kindai shakai to kirisutokyō*, 107.

What caused this change is not clear, but it coincided with several things: a change in the Japanese Protestant constituency from former samurai to white-collar urbanites,[32] public controversy between Japanese Protestant theologians (notably Ebina Danjō and Uemura Masahisa), decline in church membership, and a gradual institutionalization of the government ideology concerning the emperor and his ancestors.

To trace, or even to specify, these and related developments historically is not our present concern. The point of immediate importance is that from about 1890, Japanese Protestantism appears to have grown more accommodating than it had been.

The first generation, then, not only acknowledged the principle of non-compromise with "idol worship" but also, in many cases, put this principle into practice consistently and even aggressively. The second generation continued to acknowledge the principle, but apparently came to entertain doubts as to whether Christianity really required them to take so rigid a stand in relation to ritual remembrance of their ancestors.

THE PRESENT GENERATION: POST-FUNERAL RITES

We turn now to present-day Japanese Protestantism in order to explore the question of possible influence from the *ie* system and the custom of post-funeral liminal rites. For this part of the inquiry, I have relied partly on observation, partly on published information, and partly on 30–40 informants, most of whom live in the Tokyo-Yokohama area and belong to the Nihon Kirisuto Kyōdan, known in English as the "United Church of Christ in Japan." Given the general custom of forty-nine days of major rituals followed by incorporation into the pre-ancestral dead, then thirty-three years of linear and cyclical rites followed by incorporation into the body of ancestors, the expectation is that among Japanese Christians too there should be evidence for an extension of mortuary rites beyond the funeral.

The Protestant funeral described by Morioka shows that post-funeral rites existed as of 1887. Since then, the *ie* system has

---

[32] Ikado, "Social Status of Protestant Christianity."

grown weaker; religious freedom has grown stronger; population mobility has led to attenuation of shrine and temple connections in the populace at large; and even among Buddhist families, the rites once held every seven days during the period of primary mourning are often abbreviated to two: one on the seventh, the other on the forty-ninth day.[33] Nearly a century has passed since 1887. What about Japanese Christians today? Do they simply make their farewells at the funeral and grave, or do they engage in behavior that can be recognized as an extension of mortuary rites?

In order to answer this question, I shall consider three kinds of behavior: grave visits, memorial services, and actions relating to the mortuary tablet.

The role of the mortuary tablet in the Japanese ancestral cult tradition is central. In a sense it is the visible symbol of a spiritual presence. To it one daily offers food and drink and, as occasion affords, one presents gifts that others make to the family.[34] That something so important in the ancestral cult should have no counterpart whatever in Japanese Protestantism is almost inconceivable. What Christians are to do about this tablet, or what to substitute for it, is a problem they can hardly avoid.

One solution, chosen by a small number of informants of advanced years, is to maintain the buddha altar intact. This makes it possible to retain the tablets and remember the dead with daily food and periodic rituals. So long as this is done in the home, no problem of conscience seems to arise. The difficulty comes with the *hōji*, the rites held at the Buddhist temple with members from several linked households in attendance and with a priest as officiant. Of course even Protestants who maintain no buddha altar and no mortuary tablets occasionally participate in

---

[33] Hanayama Shōyū, *Sōshiki, hōyō, nipponkyō* [Funerals, Buddhist rites, and the religion of being Japanese] (Tokyo: Fujin Seikatsusha, 1975), 185–87.

[34] Smith, *Ancestor Worship*, 84, 90–91. For a ridiculing critique of this custom, see Hashimoto Tatsumi, *Ancestor Worship and Japanese Daily Life*, transl. by Percy T. Luke (Tokyo: Word of Life Press, 1962), 10, 23 and Obata Susumu, *Kirisutokyō keichōgaku jiten: Kon to sō* [A Christian handbook for joyful and sad occasions: Weddings and funerals] (Tokyo: Inochi no Kotoba Sha, 1978).

such rites; for the most part they regard their participation less as a religious act than as a family obligation. In this case the problem of conscience is minimal. But Protestants who maintain the mortuary tablets in the buddha altar, especially Protestants in rural, face-to-face communities, can hardy avoid calling on the Buddhist priest to conduct the periodic *hōji* ceremonies. Failure to do so would elicit severe disapproval, perhaps even ostracism. On the other hand, through the very act of calling on the Buddhist priest to conduct these rites, these village Protestants are saying that in order to remember their dead properly, they have to turn to an alternative religious institution. In principle Christianity rejects dual religious affiliation; in practice, however, a degree of dual affiliation becomes evident in this form of religious behavior. Those who maintain the mortuary tablets are involved, then, in certain necessary corollaries: the buddha altar, ceremonies at the Buddhist temple, and a de facto dual religious affiliation. How they themselves regard this behavior differs, of course, from person to person. Some find it painful. Others see in it a welcome complement to an overly narrow Christianity.[35] Among the people I have consulted, however, most seem to find dual affiliation unpalatable, for few have chosen to maintain either the buddha altar or the traditional mortuary tablet.

The alternative solution appears to be the photograph. How many generations are thus covered and how general the practice is remains to be investigated, but some Japanese Protestants seem to treat a given photograph of a deceased family member much as people in a Buddhist family treat their mortuary tablets. They keep it in a visible location, treat it protectively, present before it gifts of fruit and vegetables that come to the family, and in all probability address themselves to the person it represents, not in prayer but in speech, uttered or unuttered.

With regard to grave visits, the information presently available to me suggests that Japanese Protestants not only visit their

---

[35] Thus the old man interviewed by H. Byron Earhart in "Gedatsukai: One Life History and Its Significance for Interpreting Japanese New Religions," *Japanese Journal of Religious Studies* 7 (1980): 227–57.

family graves but also time their visits to coincide with the spring and fall equinoxes and/or with the midsummer *bon* festival period.

As for memorial services, I am informed that it is by no means unusual for members of a Christian family to ask their pastor to hold private services for a deceased family member, either at home or in the church, perhaps with a few close friends in attendance. The interesting thing is that these services, when not annual, seem to fall on or near the death anniversaries of the third, seventh, thirteenth, seventeenth, and subsequent years.[36]

If to the family-requested memorial services one adds the collective memorial services held annually by the church, often at the time of *higan* or *bon*, it becomes evident that Japanese Protestantism, both familial and ecclesiastical, includes prolonged post-funeral mortuary rites, both linear and cyclical.

THE PRESENT GENERATION: *IE* SYSTEM INFLUENCE

The institution that requires the ancestral cult is the *ie* or household system, and it has already been noted that this system serves as a prototype to which Japanese people seem to turn almost instinctively when setting up an organization. The question next to be considered, therefore, is whether Japanese Protestantism shows evidence of influence from the *ie* system.

For the purpose of considering this question, two forms of influence may be hypothesized. One is that of the main and branch household relationship, the other that of rites for the founding ancestor.

The simplest paradigm of household development is that of a married couple who, acquiring both property and progeny,

---

[36] Yamauchi, writing as a Christian pastor, recommends annual services on the death anniversaries. He goes on to suggest that if the ashes of the deceased have not yet been interred, they and/or a photograph of the deceased be placed in a central position, together with flowers and candles, at the head of a table around which survivors and friends gather. After the pastor has read a passage from the Bible, given a brief talk and led in prayer, those present, sharing tea and cakes, reminisce about the deceased. Yamauchi Rokurō, *Kirisutokyō kankon sōsai nyūmon* [A Christian introduction to rites of passage] (Tokyo: Seibunsha, 1973), 176–77. Those familiar with Buddhist *hōji* will be struck by the parallels.

bring into their house a bride for the eldest son and allot part of their wealth to help a second son build a house on family-owned land. In time the two households may be joined by a third, a non-consanguineal household set up for a devoted worker who spent many years serving the parents. In combination, the main house and the subsequently developed branch houses form a single corporate unit. The branch houses exist only because of the initial subsidy and continuing support of the main house; they are bound to it by ties of gratitude and affection, not to mention mutual support in enterprises such as agriculture, fishing, and the like. The main house is the house of the parents, or *oya*, and when the eldest son and his wife succeed them, they are known as the *oyakata*, the ones in the parental roles.

This main-branch relationship can also be found in Japanese Protestantism. When a church grows strong enough, it may decide to start a *dendōsho*, or "preaching point." Not all new churches start this way, to be sure. Some start because of the initiative of an individual Japanese Christian, lay or ordained; some because of the initiative of one or more missionaries; some because of the decision of a handful of people, already Christian but new to an area, to invite a pastor. But if a church formally decides to start a preaching point, it will allot part of its wealth and perhaps part of its human resources to this purpose. The initiating church is commonly spoken of as the *oya kyōkai* or "parent church," and the two are bound by ties remarkably similar to those of main and branch households.

Moreover, just as main and branch households experience differing fortunes, such that the power of the main house may wane while that of the branch house waxes to such an extent that they reverse roles,[37] so main and branch churches likewise experience changing relationships. Probably the most common development is that a branch church becomes a *tanritsu kyōkai*, an "independent church" equal in status to the church that was once its parent.

If nothing more were involved in this pattern of church

---

[37] Takeda, *Sosen sūhai* [Ancestor worship], 37, 82–83; Yonemura, "*Dōzoku* and Ancestor Worship," 189, 192.

growth, there would be no particular reason to link it with the ancestral rite tradition. The *ie* system as a corporate unit of main and branch entities includes, however, more than economic and structural ties. It also includes genealogical ties.

In the paradigm of household development just described, the initial couple may retire and turn management responsibilities over to their eldest son and his wife. But when the initial couple, particularly the man, dies, he becomes the founding ancestor of the entire corporate unit.[38] As such, he is made the object of periodic rites observed in common by each household in the corporation and is treated, functionally, as the chief guardian deity of the corporate entity.[39]

In the world of Japanese Christian institutions, a founder is commonly accorded a degree of ritual respect that has, so far as I know, no counterpart in United States Protestantism. A brief look at two types of institutions will make this point clear.

Among the churches that trace their origin to a specific individual, one can find several that hold, annually or at stated times, a memorial service on or near the death anniversary of the founder.[40] Others, in commemorating the day on which the institution was established, consistently emphasize the immeasurable debt of gratitude owed to the founder. On such occasions it is often the case that dependent branch churches participate in these memorial rites. It is difficult not to see both in these observances and in the participation of dependent churches a continuation of the main-branch household prototype, including its requirement of a common founding ancestor.

Among the Protestant schools, this pattern is, if anything, even more pronounced. A particularly clear example is Dōshisha University. Its founder, Niijima Jō, died January 23, 1890. His grave is located on a hill in Kyoto not far from the campus. To

---

[38] There may be a fictitious ancestor drawn from the world of myth or from the imperial line as well, but that does not concern us here.

[39] Cf. Yonemura, "*Dōzoku* and Ancestor Worship," 180.

[40] The memorial service type is exemplified by Fujimichō Church, founded by Uemura Masahisa, and Shinanomachi Church, founded by Takakura Tokutarō. The commemoration-day type is exemplified by Reinanzaka Church, founded by Kozaki Hiromichi, and Den'enchōfu Church, founded by Okada Gosaku.

this day, a graveside service is held three times each year: once on the anniversary of his death, another on the day commemorating the founding of the school, and a third at the beginning of each school year so that entering students can be "introduced" to the founder.

It appears, therefore, that both structurally and ritually, contemporary Japanese Protestantism receives important influences from the *ie* system.

CONCLUSION

With regard to the prolongation of post-funeral mortuary rites, reliance on a mortuary tablet or substitute, the main-branch relationship between churches, and the relatively strong emphasis on repeated rites for a recognized founder, Japanese Protestantism gives evidence of features that can reasonably be understood as consequences of its encounter with the Japanese cultural tradition of ancestor veneration and the household system that makes this tradition necessary.

This is not to say that Japanese Protestantism in its entirety can be comprehended from this perspective alone. The ancestral rite tradition, however important, is but one of several contending influences. Another, to mention only one, is the nationwide denominational structure as an organizational principle. In relation to this highly visible structural form, the *ie* system influence manifest in the churches lives an almost underground existence. The fact that not all churches honor their founders in the same way is probably to be explained by reference to these contending influences.

The problem with which this inquiry began, however, was to determine whether there is presumptive evidence for the existence of influence on Protestant Christianity in Japan from the ancestral cult tradition. I conclude that such evidence has been found, and that more detailed research is warranted.

Chapter 6

Japanese Christians and the Ancestors

F OR A NUMBER OF YEARS I have been interested in the question: how does a religion change as it moves from one culture to another?

My first acquaintance with this problem came from reading a study that contrasted the pre-exilic and post-exilic forms of the religion of Judaism. The author of this study (R. C. Zaehner if I remember correctly) pointed out a number of significant differences between pre- and post-exilic Judaism. Before the exile there were no angels, there was no devil, no hell as a place of punishment, no judgment after death, and no resurrection. In one stream of post-exilic Judaism, conversely, we find Satan, angels, hell as a place of punishment, judgment after death, and resurrection. Put simply, this is the difference between groups later known as the Sadducees and the Pharisees. The Sadducees in exile continued the pre-exilic traditions. The question posed by the author of this study was: how did the Pharisees come to maintain a different tradition? His answer, in brief, is that the Pharisees represent the exiled Jews who adopted certain features of the religion then dominant in ancient Persia: the religion of Zoroastrianism.[1]

---

[1] He also pointed out that the old name for the area in which Zoroastrianism was temporarily dominant was Parsi, and suggested that this is the name the Zoroastrians

Lost in the mists of history are the details of how the exiled people of Judah came into contact with representatives of Zoro-astrianism, how some of the exiles determined that certain features of the religion of Zoroaster (or Zarathustra) were admi-rable and compatible with their own way of life, how their adoption of such features affected their relationships with the more conservative group that later became known as the Sad-ducees, and the like. In order to identify theoretically useful features we can, however, begin with known facts and make a few surmises.

It is known, for example, that the people of Judah were forcibly exiled to Persia. Their contact with Zoroastrianism came, therefore, not as a result of contact with Zoroastrian "missionaries to Judah," but as a result of contact with Zoroastri-ans in a culture where the religion was already established and where they themselves were foreigners. It seems probable, more-over, that just as the Zoroastrians were then in power, so the Jewish group known as the Sadducees represented the people with links to those who had formerly been in power in Judah, people with an interest in maintaining the ancient traditions intact. By the same token, those later known as the Pharisees might represent Jewish people who formerly had little connec-tion with political or religious office and thus might be more open to influence from the Zoroastrian politico-religious elite in the new cultural setting.

The question of how a religion changes as it moves from one culture to another embraces, then, if the Jewish-Zoroastrian experience be taken as a model, a number of interrelated fea-tures: (1) the religion under consideration is a minority religion in encounter with a politically and culturally dominant majority religion; (2) the minority religion does not change in toto, but its adherents can be logically divided into two groups, one of which stands for changeless tradition, the other for changing tradition; (3) the changing tradition group presumably advances

---

carried with them when, on losing power, they fled to India, there becoming the group known today as the Parsees. He further surmised that the ancient name Parsi may have led to the name Pharisee. This feature of his argument, however, is not germane to the present inquiry.

its opportunities by adopting features of the majority religion, whereas the changeless tradition group does not; and (4) the changes noted can be characterized as ideational (i.e., changes in the realm of ideas or doctrines) — but this does not rule out the possibility that in other cultural settings the changes could be primarily in the realm of ritual behavior.

The idea of "change" necessarily implies comparison between two states. If the undertaking is diachronic, it calls for comparison between a "before" and an "after." If the undertaking is synchronic, it calls for comparison between state X and state non-X.

If a sociologist of religion in the time of the exile had attempted to study how Judaism changed in its encounter with Zoroastrianism, a diachronic approach would have led the sociologist to compare pre-exilic Judaism with exilic or post-exilic Judaism and to ask whether elements distinctive in the latter were traceable to Zoroastrianism. If the approach had been synchronic, the sociologist would have posited the existence of two logically distinct groups in exilic or post-exilic Judaism, compared each with Zoroastrianism and its culture, and asked whether the differences between the two groups could be traced to Zoroastrianism.

THE FOCUS OF THIS INQUIRY

The present inquiry is concerned with the question of how Protestant Christianity has changed since its spread from North America to Japan. It focuses on the question not of official doctrinal or liturgical change in institutional Protestantism, but on the question of how living Japanese Christians of the Nihon Kirisuto Kyōdan regard and treat the ancestors.[2] If a historical approach were feasible, it would doubtless show that the Protestant Christianity brought to Japan beginning in the 1850s,

---

[2] Since the official English name of the Nihon Kirisuto Kyōdan is "United Church of Christ in Japan," I shall refer to it as the United Church. The focus throughout is on mainline Japanese Protestants affiliated with the United Church, but in the interest of brevity I usually refer to "Japanese Christians" and "Japanese Christianity." For information on Japanese Catholics and how they regard and treat the ancestors, see Doerner, "Comparative Analysis."

though by no means identical with Puritanism, was still so strongly influenced by what we may call the "Puritan mentality" that there was no room for compromise with regard to "heathen rituals." To the extent that missionaries from North America were the "teachers" and Japanese converts the "students," it would also follow that Japanese Protestants in the early Meiji period held fast, by and large, to the Puritan mentality. We can assume that the first Japanese Protestants represented for the most part the idea of changeless tradition.

But because the scarcity of historical data concerning funerals and other rituals for the dead in mid-nineteenth-century America and Japan makes a diachronic approach unfeasible, the approach employed here will be synchronic. It compares Christian with non-Christian in present-day Japanese culture, distinguishes two groups among Christian and non-Christian Japanese depending on how they relate to their ancestors, and asks whether the differences between the Christians in these groups signify a change in Protestant Christianity.[3]

METHODOLOGICAL PARAMETERS

This inquiry relies heavily on data from a small-scale questionnaire conducted in Japan. The survey was distributed to three groups of people in urban settings: (1) church members and other people present at a United Church congregation in Kamakura on a Sunday morning in December 1986, (2) family members and acquaintances of a sizable number of people in the first group, and (3) a group of largely non-Christian people, some in Tokyo and some in Nagoya, concerned about their children's involvement in the Unification Church. Of the 969 questionnaires distributed, 514 (53.0%) were returned, but 63 (6.5%) were incompletely filled out and therefore counted as useless. Primary data are drawn from the remaining 451 questionnaires.

---

[3] The focus, therefore, is on ritual behavior and on the attitudes and possessions that relate to this behavior. In this connection the cautionary note stressed by McMullin is well worth remembering: in Asia, if not in the West, ritual is not necessarily a child of doctrine; on the contrary, doctrine often functions to make sense of ritual. Cf. Neil McMullin, "Historical and Historiographical Issues in the Study of Pre-modern Japanese Religions," *Japanese Journal of Religious Studies* 16 (1989): 29.

It will be recognized immediately that distribution of the questionnaire did not depend on a random-sampling procedure. This may seem a fatal flaw, but the position taken here is the one set forth by Glaser and Strauss, who distinguish between "theoretical sampling" and "statistical sampling." Theoretical sampling, used to discover conceptual categories, their properties and interrelationships, is for the purpose of generating theory. Statistical sampling, used to obtain factual data on distributions of people among categories, is for the purpose of verifying theory. Theory verification, for which accurate evidence is essential, requires stratified and random sampling. For generating theory, however, "A single case can indicate a general conceptual category or property; a few more cases can confirm the indication. . . . Comparative analysis requires a multitude of carefully selected cases, but the pressure is not on the sociologist to 'know the whole field' or to have all the facts 'from a careful random sample.' His job is not to provide a perfect description of an area, but to develop a theory that accounts for much of the relevant behavior."[4] Since this paper seeks to develop theory, not to verify a developed theory, I have chosen to depend not on random sampling but on theoretical sampling.

The questionnaire fashioned for this purpose was entitled *Nihonjin no shūkyō bunka ni kansuru ishiki chōsa* [A survey of Japanese people's attitudes toward religious culture]. It was designed as a multiple-choice questionnaire to be returned anonymously. There were forty-eight questions in all, forty-one of which relate to attitude, behavior, or possessions, and seven of which have to do with age, sex, education, marital status, occupation, and the like. In this article I shall not try to cover the questionnaire in its entirety, but will limit myself to the question of whether, in their relationships to the ancestors, Japanese Christians differ significantly from Japanese non-Christians or from one another.[5]

---

[4] Barney G. Glaser and Anselm S. Strauss, *The Discovery of Grounded Theory: Strategies for Qualitative Research* (New York: Aldine de Gruyter, 1967), 30; italics in original. See also pp. 62–65. I should like to express my appreciation to Dr. Mark R. Mullins of Meiji Gakuin University for calling this book to my attention.

[5] When theoretical sampling is employed, the question of how to recognize "significant difference" has to be answered differently from the way it would be answered

DIVISION AND SUBDIVISION

The first task is to divide the 451 people who turned in usable questionnaires into two groups, Christian and non-Christian. The key question for this purpose is the following: "What religion or religions do you believe in, if any?" To this question, 251 persons replied that they believe in Christianity. The remaining 200 people are counted as non-Christians. Graph 4 shows how these two groups replied to this question.

The second task is to divide the Christian respondents into two groups, depending on how they relate to their ancestors. And in order to compare similar groups, it is important to divide the non-Christian respondents in the same way. This task is not

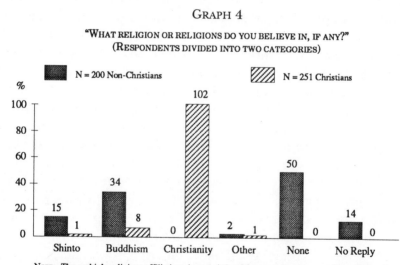

GRAPH 4

"WHAT RELIGION OR RELIGIONS DO YOU BELIEVE IN, IF ANY?"
(RESPONDENTS DIVIDED INTO TWO CATEGORIES)

NOTE: The multiple religious affiliation characteristic of Japanese people generally, a feature that theologians call "syncretism," applies to some extent to Japanese Christians as well. Nearly 10% of the Christian respondents indicate belief in a religion or religions other than Christianity. In addition, and this is the reason that the percentage of Christian respondents exceeds 100%, a smattering of the Christians say that they believe in both Protestantism and Catholicism.

in the case of statistical sampling. For statistical sampling, one would use the regular tests for standard deviation appropriate to stratified and random sampling. Theoretical sampling, however, which is more exploratory, permits a more flexible approach. Accordingly, I shall present percentages in round numbers rather than as decimals.

as easy as it would seem, for it commonly happens that the practices observed in connection with the buddha altar,[6] the traditional place for "remembering the ancestors," are carried out by one person, usually the wife, on behalf of the entire household. The question "What religion or religions do you believe in, if any?" could be answered on an individual basis, but buddha altar practices, which are frequently representative actions, do not permit answers on an individual basis. A rough division may be attempted, however, on the basis of answers to the question whether there is a buddha altar in the home. Among the 251 Christians, 25 percent said that there is a buddha altar in the home, so the remaining 75 percent are counted as having none. Among the 200 non-Christians, 43 percent said that there is a buddha altar in the home, so the remaining 57 percent are counted as having none.[7] In order to identify each of the four groups, I shall attach to each a recognizable label that makes use of the Japanese word for a buddha altar: *butsudan*. Non-Christians with an ancestral altar in the home I shall call "Japanese (with butsudan)," and those with none in the home I shall call "Japanese (no butsudan)." Christians with an ancestral altar in the home I shall call "Christian Japanese (with butsudan)" and those with none in the home I shall call "Christian Japanese (no butsudan)." Graph 5 shows how these four groups responded to the question "What religion or religions do you

---

[6] Ordinarily, the Japanese term *butsudan* is translated into English as "Buddhist altar." The connection with institutional Buddhism is not to be denied, but for most of the year an altar of this kind is the place where a household ritually remembers its ancestors. As Charles Eliot long ago pointed out in *Japanese Buddhism* (London: Routledge; New York: Barnes and Noble, 1959 [first publ. 1935], 185), Japan is unique among countries that honor the Buddhist tradition in calling any dead person *hotoke* (buddha, or "enlightened one"). Takeda (*Sosen sūhai* [Ancestor worship], 1957) maintains, in addition, that the butsudan, since it is only formally connected with Buddhism, is really a place to honor the *hotoke* of the house. (The ideograph for *hotoke* 仏 can also be read *butsu*, so the *butsudan* 仏壇 is, in practice, an altar not for the Buddha but for the household "buddhas.") Since the focus of this inquiry is not on the connection with the Buddha or with institutional Buddhism but with the household dead, I shall refer to this altar either as the "ancestral altar" or, using the Japanese term, as the butsudan.

[7] Two of the Christians gave no answer to this question, and ten of the non-Christians. They are counted as having no buddha altar in the home, but it is possible that they have one. The margin of error in the former case is 1 percent, in the latter, 5 percent.

believe in, if any?" The closer personal link with Buddhism on the part of people who belong to households with an ancestral altar will be readily apparent.[8]

GRAPH 5

"WHAT RELIGION OR RELIGIONS DO YOU BELIEVE IN, IF ANY?"
(RESPONDENTS DIVIDED INTO FOUR CATEGORIES)

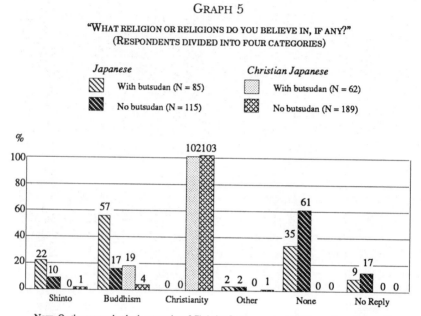

NOTE: On the reason that both categories of Christian Japanese exceed 100%, see the note to graph 7.

One stereotype has it that every "traditional" Japanese home will have an ancestral altar. Takeda (in Newell, *Ancestors*, 131) goes so far as to say that apart from nuclear families living in apartment housing in and near large cities, "all Japanese homes contain two sacred altars, one to the buddhas (*butsudan*) and one to the native gods (*kamidana*)" — almost as if *not* having an ancestral altar is a state of affairs so exceptional that it can safely be ignored. In fact, however, much depends on whether a household is rural or urban, how long it has existed in its present location, and whether it is multi-generational. (*cont. on p. 129*)

---

[8] With regard to belief in Buddhism, graph 8 shows a 40% difference between the two groups of non-Christian Japanese (those with and those without a butsudan), and a 15 percent difference between the two comparable groups of Christian Japanese.

Photo 2: *A rather elaborate butsudan (buddha altar) in the home of a well-to-do family. The light-colored statue at the center is a figure of Kannon, the bodhisattva of mercy. Before it, and slightly to the left, is a lacquered* ihai *(mortuary tablet) inscribed with Chinese characters. Other* ihai *may be seen further to the left. On the right is a small statue of a Buddhist priest, perhaps the founder of their sect. On the table, flanked by flowers, is a teacup and two other cups: one for rice, the other for a cooked vegetable. Gifts to the family (fresh fruit and boxed gifts) are first shared with the ancestors, then enjoyed by the rest of the family.*

Photo 3: *A kamidana (kami altar) and butsudan arranged side by side. The kami altar (on the left) is made of plain, unpainted wood. Complete with roof, pillars, and doors, it is shaped like a small house.*

The buddha altar displays a photo of a deceased family member. On each side of the photo are inscribed tablets of plain wood. The shorter of the two is a temporary mortuary tablet. On the table are an incense bowl, a rice bowl, candles, a bell, and a striker to tap it with, together with fresh fruits and various gifts.

Photo 4: *A simple kami altar located just below the ceiling in the corner of a room. The unpainted miniature shrine is decorated with a symbol of the sacred: a* shimenawa *(straw plaited into a rope) from which* gohei *(paper strips in a zigzag pattern) are suspended. The talisman on the left is from Izumo Shrine.*

Dore (1958) found that 80 percent of the households in one section of Tokyo had butsudan; Sano (1958), for another section of Tokyo, found that 63 percent had one; Morioka (1970), in still another part of Tokyo, discovered that only 45 percent had butsudan (all cited in Smith, *Ancestor Worship*, 88). The survey on which the present inquiry relies shows that 43 percent of the non-Christian respondents come from homes with a butsudan. This finding is quite close to that of Morioka and probably reflects the fact that most respondents come from neolocal, urban, one- or two-generation families.[9]

Another stereotype has it that no "traditional" Christian Japanese home will have a butsudan. The present inquiry shows, however, that 25 percent of the Christian respondents belong to households that *do* have one.[10] To some Christian Japanese, particularly those without a butsudan, this may seem improper,

---

[9] No data are available as to length of residence or family composition, but to a question asking about current place of residence, the respondents' answers (in percentages) are as follows:

TABLE 7

RESPONDENTS CLASSIFIED BY PLACE OF RESIDENCE

Current Place of Residence	Christian $N=251$	Non-Christian $N=200$
1. Tokyo or Osaka	18	28
2. Tokyo or Osaka environs	45	29
3. A city of at least 500,000	9	8
4. A city of at least 100,000	19	17
5. A city of less than 100,000	6	8
6. A town or village	3	11

In round numbers, 63 percent of the Christians live in Tokyo, Osaka, or their environs, as do 57 percent of the non-Christians. Of those who live in areas classified as cities, the Christians number 35 percent and the non-Christians 33 percent. Respondents who live in towns or villages come to 11 percent among the non-Christians and a mere 3 percent among the Christians.

[10] This is not to say that all 25 percent belong to, or were raised in, Christian homes. To those who identified themselves as Christians, the question was raised, "Were you raised in a Christian home?" Of those living in a household with an ancestral altar, 69 percent said no, 7 percent said yes, and 24 percent gave no reply. (For other Christians, the percentages were 60%, 32%, and 8% respectively.)

perhaps even so shameful that they could wish that it not become public knowledge — especially for people in other countries. This attitude is probably strongest among people who understand butsudan rituals under the heading of "ancestor worship." My own attitude is somewhat different. From the angle of semantic history Takeda (1973) mentions that the Japanese term for ancestor worship, *sosen sūhai*, is not "natural" to Japan but was coined to accommodate a Western import. And from the angle of behavioral content, Fujii (in a lecture at Tokyo Union Theological Seminary in June 1989) observed that present-day Japanese anthropologists of religion no longer use this term. They now tend to use more neutral terms such as "ancestral ceremonies" (*sosen girei*) or "ancestral rites" (*sosen saishi*). Both scholars thus suggest that the term "ancestor worship" is not really adequate to describe what goes on in Japan.[11] Whether it is proper for Christian Japanese families to have a butsudan is finally a matter that Japanese pastors and theologians will be expected to determine on behalf of the church, but whatever they eventually decide will doubtless require factual knowledge as to the present state of affairs.

To anyone engaged in the study of religion and society, it is not surprising to learn that a religion, as it moves from one culture to another, takes on some features of the new culture. Since the socialization process humanizes people by providing them not only with patterns of expected behavior but also with the very categories they think and act with, the surprising thing would be for a religion that survives in a new cultural setting *not* to change in directions suggested by the socialization process.

At any rate the focus here is not on what is proper or improper, but on whether distinguishing between Christians who live in households with a butsudan and those who do not can be a theoretically useful basis for analysis of change in Protestant Christianity. The closer personal link with Buddhism on the part of people who belong to households with a butsudan

---

[11] Not all scholars of Japanese religion agree with this view, and important insights can be found in recent books that still make use of this term. See, for example, Yanagawa Keiichi, ed., *Seminā shūkyōgaku kōgi* [A seminar concerning (Professor Yanagawa's) lectures on religious studies] (Kyoto: Hōzōkan, 1988), 152–65.

has already been pointed out. Among the non-Christian Japanese, people living in households with a butsudan are three times more likely to believe in Buddhism than people living in households with no butsudan; but among the Christian Japanese, people living in households with a butsudan are five times more likely to believe in Buddhism than people living in households without one. This difference among Christian Japanese is enough to suggest that the categorical division between people who live in households with a butsudan and those who do not may indeed prove theoretically fruitful. It remains to be seen whether this is true.

TIMES PEOPLE THINK OF THE DEAD

One question people were asked had to do with when they think about the dead. Not surprisingly, almost nobody replied that they never do so. When it comes to the times that they think about the dead, however, certain differences emerge. Graph 6 shows how people answered this multiple-choice question.

The full form of the first answer to this question is "During my daily work, I sometimes catch myself thinking about the dead." The 25 percent difference between Japanese and Christian Japanese with a butsudan, and the 26 percent difference between Japanese and Christian Japanese with no butsudan, are equally striking. This sizable difference between Christian and non-Christian, together with the negligible 7 percent difference between the two categories of Christian Japanese, suggests that an ancestor-related version of the Protestant work ethic is still very much alive among Japanese Christians. This hypothesis may well be worth examining in detail on some other occasion. But the point to note here is that the existence or non-existence of an ancestral altar in the home has no connection with whether Christian Japanese think about the dead during their daily work. In either case they are more likely to do so than the non-Christian Japanese.

When it comes to the remaining answers, however, a different pattern emerges. In each case Japanese and Christian Japanese who live in households with a butsudan show a higher profile than their "no butsudan" counterparts. Among Christian Japanese, the contrast is particularly strong in relation to *higan,* the spring and autumn weeks of Buddhist services for the dead, and *bon,* the summer Festival for the Dead.

What are we to make of all this? The main difference between the "daily work" answer and the remaining answers is that the former has no particular connection with household or community rituals conventionally associated with Buddhism (not necessarily with Buddhist doctrine), whereas the latter do. It would seem, therefore, that *Christians with a butsudan in the home participate more fully in household and community rituals for the dead than Christians with no butsudan in the home.*

GRAPH 6

"AT WHAT TIMES DO YOU THINK ABOUT THE DEAD?"

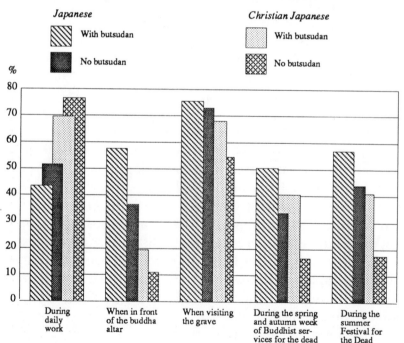

There is no reason to maintain that this difference is caused by the presence or absence of an ancestral altar in the home, but it begins to appear that this factor can usefully serve as a window that permits this difference to come into view.

OTHER RELIGIOUS OBJECTS IN THE HOME

If a household has an ancestral altar, the chances that it also has religious objects from other religious traditions would seem fairly strong. Graph 7 shows the percentage responses to the question: "Of the following objects, which ones exist in the house you now live in?"

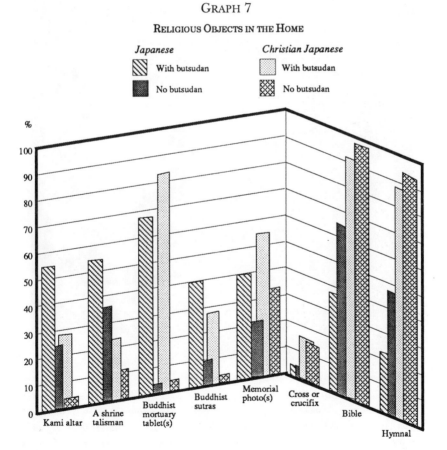

GRAPH 7

RELIGIOUS OBJECTS IN THE HOME

The left-hand panel of graph 7 demonstrates a consistent pattern. In each case Japanese and Christian Japanese people who live in households with an ancestral altar are more likely to have the object indicated than their "no butsudan" counterparts. The most striking difference occurs in connection with the *ihai*, or Buddhist mortuary tablet. Only a handful of people in households without a butsudan have such mortuary tablets. By far the strongest tendency is for people who have Buddhist mortuary

Photo 5: *A small butsudan specially decorated for the bon festival when the spirits of the dead are welcomed home for a visit. Before the photos is an ihai (mortuary tablet), and before the ihai is a bowl in which to burn incense. At left front are some fresh fruits and vegetables, and in the tray at the center are some dishes of cooked rice and other foods, together with chopsticks.*

tablets to maintain (or obtain) a butsudan in which to have the tablets ritually installed.

The right-hand panel, on the other hand, shows a somewhat less consistent pattern. Christian Japanese in households with a butsudan are somewhat more likely to have a cross or crucifix in the home than other Christian Japanese, but when it comes to a Bible or hymnal, it is the other way round. It is also noteworthy that non-Christian Japanese in households without a butsudan are more likely to have a Bible or hymnal than other non-Christian Japanese.

Apart from the specifically Christian items indicated in the right-hand panel, it appears, then, that Japanese and Christian Japanese people living in households with an ancestral altar report approximately similar patterns of religious object possession. The converse also obtains. Japanese and Christian Japanese people living in households with no ancestral altar also report generally similar patterns of religious object possession.

What we see exhibited here, I think, is not one basic pattern but two: one exemplified by the reports of non-Christian Japanese people living in households with an ancestral altar and one exemplified by the reports of non-Christian Japanese people living in households with none. In the case of those living in households with an ancestral altar, we find a comparatively high incidence of possession of a kami altar, a shrine talisman, Buddhist mortuary tablet(s), Buddhist sutras, and memorial photos. In the case of those living in households with no ancestral altar, we find a comparatively low incidence of possession of each. It is not that comparatively high incidence of possession is "normal" and comparatively low incidence "exceptional," but that there are two normal patterns: one for households that have experienced death in the family, and another for households that have not.

If the number of households always remained constant, one would expect that households possessing ancestral altars and other religious objects would gradually increase and that households of the other type would correspondingly decrease. But since the number of nuclear families is always increasing, it is normal for the two patterns to coexist—despite the movement of some households, when a death occurs, from the "no butsudan" category to the "with butsudan" category.

This basic twofold pattern inferred from the answers of the non-Christian Japanese respondents has its counterpart in a similar twofold pattern that obtains among the Christian Japanese respondents. Here too we find that in the case of those living in households with an ancestral altar, there is a comparatively high incidence of possession of the religious objects listed above. Conversely, in the case of those living in households with no ancestral altar, the incidence of possession of these objects is comparatively low.

With regard to religious objects in the home it appears, then, that the basic twofold pattern found in the homes of non-Christian Japanese respondents is repeated in the homes of Christian Japanese respondents—if generally in somewhat less pronounced form. It will be interesting to see if this parallelism occurs in other areas.

SENSE OF CONNECTION WITH THE ANCESTORS

Another question raised in the questionnaire had to do with people's sense of connection with the ancestors. The translated form of the question is this: "Are there times when you feel closely connected to your ancestors?" Graph 8 shows the relevant responses.

Of those who feel from time to time a close sense of connection with the ancestors, the majority tend to live in households that have a butsudan, but those who live in households with no butsudan are not far behind. Of those who claim never to have felt a close sense of connection with the ancestors, people living in households with no butsudan predominate.[12]

In their answers to this question, then, Japanese and Chris-

---

[12] The well-known NHK survey of Japanese religious consciousness, conducted in November 1981, showed that 59% of 2,692 respondents said that they feel a deep sense of connection with the ancestors, as opposed to 31% who said that they feel no such connection. See NHK Yoron Chōsabu, ed., *Nihonjin no shūkyō ishiki* [The religious consciousness of the Japanese people] (Tokyo: Nippon Hōsō Shuppan Kyōkai, 1984). These figures are roughly comparable to those for the "with butsudan" groups and the "no butsudan" groups in the present inquiry.

GRAPH 8

SENSE OF CONNECTION WITH THE ANCESTORS

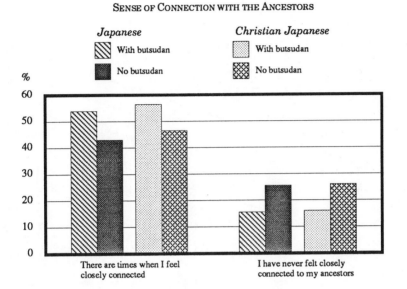

tian Japanese living in households with a butsudan demonstrate almost identical patterns—as do those in households with no butsudan. Here again we see that the pattern of the "with butsudan" households, whether Japanese or Christian Japanese, is one thing and that of the "no butsudan" households another.

THE BUTSUDAN AND THE MEMORIAL PHOTO

As already seen in graph 7, some 40 percent of the non-Christian Japanese respondents living in households with a butsudan indicated that there were memorial photos in the home as well. As for Christian Japanese respondents living in households with a butsudan, over 53 percent said that memorial photos were present. Keeping this coexistence in mind, we next examine the question of what happens before the butsudan and/or memorial photo. Graph 9 presents comparative data on the former, graph 10 on the latter.

"If there is a butsudan in the house where you currently reside (university students should answer with reference to their

GRAPH 9

WHAT HAPPENS BEFORE THE BUTSUDAN

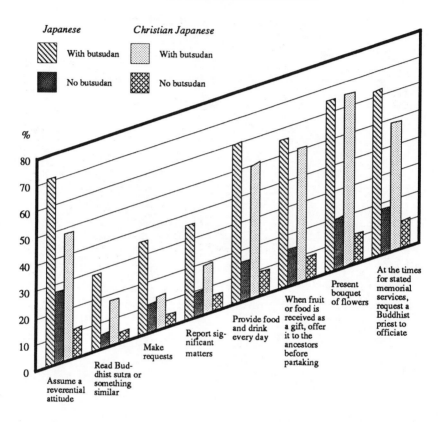

parental home), what kinds of butsudan-related behavior occur there?" This is the question with which graph 9 is concerned.

The logical puzzle here is how "no butsudan" respondents, whether Japanese or Christian Japanese, could report on what happens before the butsudan in their house at all. But setting this problem aside, we find again that the behavior reported by "with butsudan" Christian Japanese differs from the behavior reported by "no butsudan" Christian Japanese in much the same way that the behavior reported by "with butsudan" Japanese differs from the behavior reported by "no butsudan" Japanese.

GRAPH 10

WHAT HAPPENS BEFORE THE MEMORIAL PHOTO

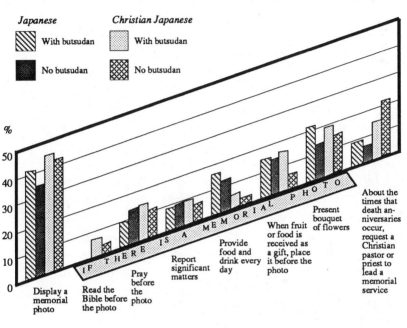

In general, the Christian Japanese report, for their houses, lower degrees of these forms of behavior than their Japanese counterparts. But particularly in relation to the last four items (providing daily food and drink, offering to the ancestors fruit or food received as a gift, presenting a bouquet of flowers, and requesting a Buddhist priest to officiate at stated memorial services), there is a pronounced tendency for the "with butsudan" Christian Japanese to report household behavior which approximates that reported by "with butsudan" Japanese.

The question graph 10 addresses is this: "Even if there is no butsudan in the house where you currently reside (university students should answer with reference to their parental home), in what ways are the dead remembered?" This question, and its multiple-choice answers, mistakenly assumed that households with no butsudan might make use of memorial photos instead — and that this substitution would be particularly evident in the Christian households. What we find in graph 10, however, is that an average of approximately 40 percent of the respondents in all four categories indicate that the memorial photo is used in their households.

As for what happens in connection with this photo, Japanese and Christian Japanese are most alike, whether or not there is a butsudan in their home, in indicating that people pray before the photo and report significant matters there. Not surprisingly, none of the non-Christian Japanese reported that people in their households read the Bible before the memorial photo. For the last four items in graph 9, Christian Japanese with a butsudan in the home reported household behavior that approximates that of the "with butsudan" Japanese.

Of the last four items in graph 10, however, this pattern holds good for only two: placing before the photo fruit or food received as a gift, and presenting a bouquet of flowers. As compared with the Christian respondents, the non-Christian respondents report that food and drink are more likely to be set before the photo every day. But when it comes to requesting a pastor or priest to lead a memorial service, it is only natural that the Christian respondents, and especially the "no butsudan" Christian respondents, report that this is more likely to occur in their homes than the non-Christian respondents report for their homes.

All in all, it seems significant that when the issue is what happens before the butsudan, the "traditional" place for ritual behavior concerned with the ancestors, then the degree of practice for a given type of behavior as reported by Christian Japanese with a butsudan in the home stands in fairly sharp contrast to the degree reported by Christian Japanese with no butsudan in the home. But when we have to do with what happens before the memorial photo, which is by no means widely accepted as a substitute place for ritual behavior concerned with the ancestors, the contrast between what these two groups of Christians report about household behavior diminishes almost to the vanishing point.

It appears, therefore, that the presence or absence of a butsudan in the home has a definite bearing on the home environment of Christian Japanese with regard to how they relate to their ancestors. Whether the presence or absence of a butsudan in the home has any bearing on Christian Japanese behavior in other areas is another matter. This is the problem to be examined next.

RELIGIOUS BEHAVIOR

Questionnaires concerned with religious attitudes and behavior and intended for people in societies where the Christian tradition is relatively deep-rooted often include questions as to frequency of church attendance, Bible reading, and prayer. Such questions are generally regarded as useless in a country like Japan, but perhaps they can be useful when put to Japanese Christians.

The result to be inferred from graph 11 is readily apparent. With regard to church attendance, Bible reading, and prayer, the presence or absence of an ancestral altar in the home makes no significant difference whatever in the lives of Christian Japanese.

Relatively frequent church attendance, Bible reading, and prayer constitute "expected behavior" in the Christian world. In the world of Japanese culture generally, however, there are other forms of expected behavior. One of the questions posed to respondents was this: "Of the actions listed below, how many do you yourself customarily perform?" The results are shown in graph 12.

As graph 12 shows, Japanese and Christian Japanese respondents differ most in relation to the third and fourth items. The non-Christian respondents are far more likely to pray for "tangible benefits" and to visit a Shinto shrine or Buddhist temple at the turn of the year than the Christian respondents.[13]

---

[13] A *Yomiuri Shimbun* newspaper survey summarized by Fujii showed that 31 percent of the respondents prayed for such "tangible benefits" and that 56 percent visited

GRAPH 11

FREQUENCY OF CHURCH ATTENDANCE, BIBLE READING, AND PRAYER
ON THE PART OF CHRISTIAN JAPANESE

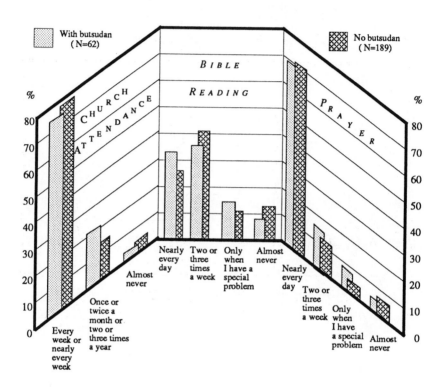

In the matter of taking a newborn child to the local Shinto shrine, the Christians move somewhat closer to the non-Christians. But it is in their responses to the second item that Japanese and Christian Japanese are closest.[14] The "with butsudan" Japanese set the pace for the "with butsudan" Christian Japanese, and the "no butsudan" Japanese for the "no butsudan"

---

a Shinto shrine or Buddhist temple at the turn of the year. Cf. Fujii, "Shūkyō kōdō" [Religious behavior], 135.

[14] With regard to visits to the family grave once or twice a year, the *Yomiuri Shimbun* survey found that 69% of the respondents do so. Cf. Fujii, "Shūkyō kōdō" [Religious behavior], 135.

GRAPH 12

"OF THE ACTIONS LISTED, WHICH ONES DO YOU CUSTOMARILY PERFORM?"

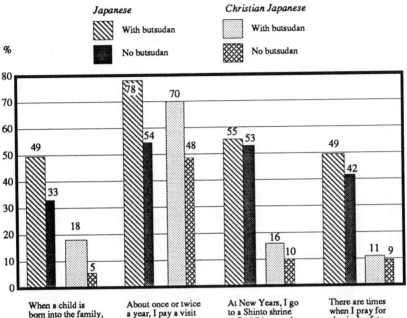

Japanese

⬜ With butsudan

◼ No butsudan

Christian Japanese

⬜ With butsudan

⬜ No butsudan

Christian Japanese. Here again it appears, therefore, that Christian Japanese correspond most closely to non-Christian Japanese in matters pertaining to the ancestors. Where the ancestors are involved, as in visits to the family grave, the difference between the Japanese and Christian Japanese "with butsudan" groups, on the one hand, and between the Japanese and Christian Japanese "no butsudan" groups, on the other, dwindles to insignificance.

This does not mean, however, that in their performance of culturally expected acts, the differences between "with butsudan" and "no butsudan" Christians are insignificant. When these groups are compared, they turn out to be most alike in not praying for physical safety, for business success, for passing grades or the like (here they differ by 2 percent), and in not going to a Shinto shrine or Buddhist temple at the turn of the year (in this case they differ by 6 percent). A perceptible 13 percent difference emerges with regard to taking a newborn child to the local Shinto shrine.[15] When it comes to family grave visits, however, a substantial 22 percent difference appears, the "with butsudan" Christian Japanese standing closer to other Japanese than to the "no butsudan" Christians.

For both groups of Christians, grave visits are obviously important, but they are especially important to Christians who belong to households with an ancestral altar.

POLITICAL ORIENTATION

The political climate in Japan has changed considerably since the time this questionnaire was distributed (December 1986),

---

[15] It may seem strange that *any* Christian would take a newborn child to the local Shinto shrine, since this act means, according to folk religion scholars, that a family introduces the infant to the shrine kami and entreats its protection for this new member of the "parish." One must immediately add, however, that few people, Japanese or Christian Japanese, think of this meaning when observing this convention — if, indeed, they are even aware of it.

Equally important, there is a clear division of opinion among Japanese people, both Christian and non-Christian, as to whether Shrine Shinto is to be understood as a religion. One of the questions put to respondents deals with this issue. Table 8 shows the percentage responses.

TABLE 8

PERCENTAGE RESPONSES TO THE QUESTION, "DO YOU AGREE WITH THE OPINION THAT WHEREAS 'RELIGION' INCLUDES BUDDHISM, CHRISTIANITY, AND MANY OTHER RELIGIONS, THE ORDINARY SHINTO SHRINE AND ITS FESTIVALS DO NOT FALL INTO THIS CATEGORY?"

	Japanese		Christian Japanese	
	With butsudan $N=85$	No butsudan $N=115$	With butsudan $N=62$	No butsudan $N=189$
Agree	34	37	37	43
Disagree	34	37	32	44
Can't say either way	19	19	21	10
Don't know/ No reply	13	9	10	2

and at least one of the parties then in existence has disappeared from the scene. But if we divide the parties of that day into right-wing and left-wing groups, it is possible, as shown in graph 13, to get a rough idea of the political orientation of Japanese and Christian Japanese in the "with butsudan" and "no butsudan" categories.

In terms of percentage support for left-wing parties, the Christian Japanese generally outnumber other Japanese, and within these two groups, the "no butsudan" Christian Japanese outnumber the "no butsudan" Japanese by about 15 percent. Among those who support right-wing parties, on the other hand, the "with butsudan" respondents, Japanese and Christian Japanese alike, outnumber their "no butsudan" counterparts by an average of 10 percent.

Among the Christian respondents, supporters of left-wing parties roughly balance the supporters of right-wing parties.

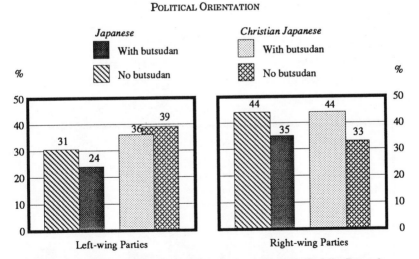

GRAPH 13

POLITICAL ORIENTATION

NOTE: The groups here classified as "left-wing" are the Japan Socialist Party, the Kōmeitō, the Japan Communist Party, and the Social Democratic Federation. The groups classified as "right-wing" are the Liberal-Democratic Party, the New Liberal Club (now defunct), and the Democratic Socialist Party.

The difference between the "with butsudan" and "no butsudan" groups is not pronounced.

With regard to political orientation, therefore, it must be concluded that the presence or absence of an ancestral altar in the home makes no discernible difference.

SUPPORT FOR THE EMPEROR SYSTEM

Since the death of Emperor Shōwa in January 1989, the question of whether to support the emperor system has been raised in many quarters. Awareness of this issue is doubtless much stronger today than it was when the questionnaire for this inquiry was distributed. The questionnaire did include, however, one question having to do with support for versus opposition to the emperor system. The responses to this question are shown in graph 14.

Not surprisingly, the preponderant percentages are on the side of those who support the emperor system. Those who support it unconditionally, whether Japanese or Christian Japanese, hover around the 10 percent line. Among those who

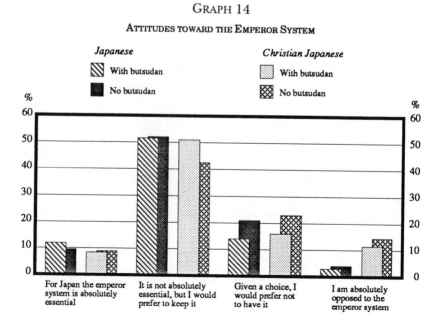

GRAPH 14

ATTITUDES TOWARD THE EMPEROR SYSTEM

support it as a matter of preference, however, it is interesting to observe that Christian Japanese who live in households where there is an ancestral altar are almost indistinguishable from other Japanese respondents—though "no butsudan" Christian Japanese trail only a short way behind.

Among those who oppose the emperor system as a matter of preference, it is interesting to note that the "no butsudan" groups, both Japanese and Christian Japanese, perceptibly over-top the "with butsudan" groups. And among those who oppose it absolutely, the proportion of Christian Japanese exceeds that of other Japanese by approximately 10 percent.

The most striking differences among the Christian Japanese occur not at the extremes but in relation to the preference items. The differences are not great, but perhaps it is no mere coincidence that Christians who live in a household where there is an ancestral altar tend to support the emperor system more than other Christian Japanese, just as Christians who live in a household where there is no ancestral altar tend to oppose it more than other Christian Japanese.

CONCLUSION

In general terms, the Christian Japanese from households with and without an ancestral altar are most *similar* in respect of frequency of church attendance, Bible reading, and prayer. They are also quite similar to each other in the degree to which they think about the dead during their daily work, in household possession of a Bible and hymnal, in *not* praying for tangible benefits and in *not* going to a Shinto shrine or Buddhist temple at New Years, and—with reference to the memorial photo—in reporting that people in their household read the Bible before the photo, pray before it, and report significant matters there.[16]

---

[16] The memorial photo can perhaps best be understood as a non-standard locus for ritual behavior relating to the ancestors. The fact that differences between the two groups of Christian Japanese become almost indiscernible where the memorial photo is involved probably reflects its ambiguous status.

Conversely, they *differ* most from each other in the degree to which they believe in Buddhism alongside Christianity, in the degree to which they think about the dead during *bon* and *higan*, in household possession of a kami altar, of Buddhist mortuary tablets, Buddhist sutras, and memorial photos, and in frequency of family grave visits. In each of these cases the Christians from households with an ancestral altar chalk up higher marks than Christians from households with no ancestral altar.[17]

These areas of similarity and difference can generally be characterized as "behavior generally expected of Christians" and "culturally expected behavior" respectively. The fact that Christian Japanese, whether from households with an ancestral altar or not, attend church, read the Bible, and pray with almost identical frequency will surprise no one. It is surprising, however, to learn that there are striking differences between these two groups of Christian Japanese in the area of culturally expected behavior.

What calls for explanation in this context is not similarity but difference. The interesting thing about the contrast found among the two groups of Christian Japanese is that it is virtually a mirror image of the twofold pattern found among the non-Christian Japanese. Where Christian Japanese from households with and without an ancestral altar differ from each other, their differences tend to approximate the differences among non-Christian Japanese from households with and without an ancestral altar. It appears, therefore, that the two patterns that normally occur in present-day Japanese society, one for households with an ancestral altar and the other for households with none, serve as models for ancestor-related behavior among Christian Japanese in the area of culturally expected behavior. In this area it is through comparison with the ancestor-related behavior of present-day non-Christian Japanese that the differences between Christian Japanese need to be understood.

---

[17] In respect of political orientation and attitude toward the emperor system, we found a slight tendency toward conservatism on the part of Christian Japanese from households with an ancestral altar (as opposed to those from households with none), but no pronounced differences were observed. Accordingly, these matters need not be considered further.

This inquiry began with the question whether Protestant Christianity has changed through contact with Japanese culture. If the assumption is correct that the Protestantism that first came to Japan was so deeply imbued with the Puritan mentality that it would have nothing to do with ancestral rituals beyond the funeral, it follows that mainline Protestantism as found in Japan today has changed considerably. The analysis does not show that Christian Japanese can be divided into a "changeless tradition group" and a "changing tradition group" (into "Sadducees" and "Pharisees"). It shows, rather, that in the area of culturally expected behavior, both Christians from households with an ancestral altar and those from households with none have changed in such a way that their differences tend to correspond to the differences found among the same two groups of non-Christian Japanese.

It has also been shown, I believe, that the analytical division of Christian Japanese into those coming from households with and without an ancestral altar opens up data hitherto unrecognized. It is to be hoped that this type of analysis will prove fruitful in future research.

Chronology,
Bibliography,
Index & Glossary

Chronology of Japanese Social and Religious History

YAYOI PERIOD (200 B.C.E.–250 C.E.)

c. 239   The Chinese *Wei Chih* gives the first surviving written account of the people of Wa (Japan) and the female shaman Himiko (or Pimiko) who helped her younger brother rule the country.

TUMULUS PERIOD (250–500)

400–500   Approximate period Yamato establishes superiority over other clans; special sites set aside for ruler-performed rituals.

EARLY HISTORY (500–1185)

ASUKA PERIOD (552–646)

513   Confucian scholars arrive from Korea.

538 (or 552)   Official introduction of Buddhism from Korea.

552   Epidemics rage. Members of the Mononobe clan destroy Buddhist images and raze Buddhist temples. Some say that this year, the first after the 1500 years since the Buddha's death, marks the beginning of the eschatological *mappō*, the last, degenerating period of history.

585 Soga-no-Umako, head of one of the leading clans and a devotee of Buddhism, erects a pagoda and ritually installs a relic of the Buddha. The Mononobe and Nakatomi clans again destroy Buddhist temples and images.

593 Prince Shōtoku becomes regent to Empress Suiko.

603 Prince Shōtoku institutes a twelve-rank system for court officials (later reduced to eight ranks).

604 Prince Shōtoku, guided by Buddhism and Confucianism, issues the Seventeen-Article Constitution and adopts the Chinese calendar.

607 Construction begins on Hōryū-ji Temple.

625 The Korean priest Hui-kuan (Jps., Ekan) introduces the Jōjutsu and Sanron schools of Buddhism.

646 Proclamation of the Taika Reforms.

657 Beginning of the *bon* festival in Japan.

661 The Japanese priest Dōshō, after study in China, introduces the Hossō school.

n.d. Chitsū and Chidatsu, after study in China, introduce the Kusha school and the second wave of Hossō doctrine.

685 Beginning of the practice of alternating the sites of the Grand Shrine of Ise, rebuilding the shrine anew every twenty years.

699 En-no-Gyōja, legendary founder of Shugendō, is exiled to Izu.

700 First cremation in Japan. Dōshō, the person cremated, is a Buddhist monk of the Hossō school.

701 The Taihō Code is promulgated with *ritsu* (penal) and *ryō* (administrative) directives and with provisions regulating the ranks assigned to Buddhist monks and nuns.

703 First imperial cremation: the Empress Jitō.

NARA PERIOD (710–794)

710 First fixed capital established at Nara.

712 Compilation of the *Kojiki* (Record of ancient matters).

718 The Yōrō Code revises the provisions of the Taihō Code.

720   Compilation of the *Nihongi*, also known as the *Nihonshoki* (Chronicles of Japan).

733   Compilation of the *Izumo fudoki* (Description of the Izumo region).

736   The Chinese priest Tao-hsüan (Jps., Dōsen) introduces the doctrines of the Kegon school.

740   The Korean priest Shen-hsiang (Jps., Shinjō) founds the Kegon school in Japan.

741 or 738   Edict of the Emperor Shōmu that state-supported temples (*kokubun-ji*) and nunneries (*kokubun ni-ji*) be established in each province, with Kegon sect Tōdai-ji Temple in Nara as the parent temple. The monk Gyōgi, renowned among common people for initiating construction of bridges and dikes, is enlisted to win support for this enterprise.

749   Completion of the statue of the Vairocana Buddha for Tōdai-ji Temple.

n.d.   Completion of the *Man'yōshū* (Collection of myriad leaves).

754   The Chinese monk Chien-chên (Jps., Ganjin) introduces the Ritsu discipline.

788   Saichō founds on Mt. Hiei what later becomes Enryaku-ji Temple.

HEIAN PERIOD (794–1160)

794   Capital transferred to Kyoto (then called Heiankyō).

804   Emperor sends Saichō to China for study.

805   Saichō returns and founds the Tendai school.

806   Kūkai returns from two years of study in China and founds the Shingon school.

816   Kūkai establishes Kongōbu-ji Temple on Mt. Kōya.

823   Approximate date of completion of the *Nihon ryōiki*, the first collection of Buddhist tales in Japan.

n.d.   Kūkai completes the *Jūjūshin ron* (Treatise on the ten stages of spiritual development) sometime between 824 and 833.

859 Enryaku-ji Temple priest Eryō, in his *Sandai jitsuroku*, advances an early version of the *honji suijaku* theory (the theory that Shinto kami, though avatars of bodhisattvas, are still no more than potential buddhas and therefore in need of enlightenment). Acceptance of this theory grows slowly during the next four centuries.

894 Discontinuance of the practice of sending imperial envoys to China.

927 The *Engishiki*, embodying a code of Shinto rituals, brings Shinto into the legal system.

938 The monk Kūya enters the capital and begins to preach Amida piety.

981 Armed struggle between the priests of Enryaku-ji and Onjō-ji temples marks the emergence of the *sōhei* or soldier-monk.

985 Completion of Genshin's *Ōjōyōshū* (Essentials of rebirth).

1008 Approximate date of completion of Murasaki Shikibu's *Genji monogatari* (Tale of Genji) and Sei Shōnagon's *Makura no sōshi* (Pillow book).

1052 Widely believed to be the year that ushers in the last, degenerating period of history when Buddhism exists only as an abstract teaching, not as a way of life; eschatological ideas (*mappō shisō*) prevail.

TAIRA PERIOD (1160–1185)

1175 Hōnen finds enlightenment in Amida pietism and begins to teach "the one way left." The Pure Land sect dates from this time.

MEDIEVAL PERIOD (1185–1868)

KAMAKURA PERIOD (1185–1333)

1185 Minamoto Yoritomo, lord of Kamakura, receives permission from the Imperial Court to appoint law-enforcement officers and revenue collectors through Japan. This step marks the transfer of political power from Kyoto to Kamakura.

1191 Eisai, after study in China, returns to found the Rinzai sect of Zen Buddhism.

1192 Yoritomo, named *Seii-tai-shōgun* ("barbarian-subduing generalissimo") with authority from the emperor, becomes military dictator and begins the Kamakura shogunate.

1194 At the behest of Enryaku-ji Temple monks, the propagation of Zen Buddhism is suppressed.

1198 Hōnen completes the charter document of the Japanese Pure Land sect, his two-volume *Senchaku hongan nenbutsu shū* (Treatise on selecting the *nenbutsu* of the original vow). Eisai completes his three-volume *Kōzen gokoku ron* (Zen growth for the protection of the country), the first book on Zen Buddhism produced in Japan.

n.d. Zen priests returning from Sung China introduce Chu Hsi Neo-Confucianism early in the Kamakura period.

1200 Kamakura shogunate bans the practice of Amida pietism.

1201 Shinran becomes a disciple of Hōnen.

1207 Hōnen is exiled to Tosa province, Shinran to Echigo province. Both pardoned in 1211.

1219 Approximate date of completion of the *Heike monogatari* (Tale of the Heike).

1224 Approximate date of Shinran's completion of his six-volume *Kyōgyōshinshō* (Teaching, practice, faith, and attainment). The True Pure Land sect begins.

   Shogunate suppresses those who advocate or practice Amida pietism as the only way left.

1227 Dōgen returns from four years of study in China and founds the Sōtō sect of Zen Buddhism. Soldier-monks of Enryaku-ji Temple demolish Hōnen's burial place and burn the woodcut printing blocks for his *Senchaku hongan nenbutsu shū*.

1243 Dōgen establishes Eihei-ji Temple in Echizen province.

1253 Nichiren begins to preach *Lotus Sūtra* faith. The Nichiren sect dates from this time.

   Dōgen completes his *Shōbō genzō* (Collection of essays on the true dharma).

1260   Nichiren writes the *Risshō ankoku ron* (Restore the right teaching and achieve security for our country), insisting that foreign invasion will follow if Japan does not abandon false forms of Buddhism and adopt *Lotus Sūtra* faith. He submits it as a petition to the Kamakura shogunate.

1271   Nichiren is exiled to Sado Island. Pardoned in 1273.

1274   Khubilai, Mongol emperor of Yüan China, dispatches troops to Hakata Bay in northern Kyushu in an effort to force Japan to accept a tributary relationship. Bad weather and military losses force them to retreat to Korea. Kamakura shogunate begins erecting fortifications around Hakata Bay.

1276   Ippen, a missionary of Amida pietism, begins what later becomes the Ji sect.

1279   Ippen begins the *odori nenbutsu* (ecstatic dancing while chanting "Namu Amida Butsu" [I take refuge in Amida Buddha]).

1281   Khubilai dispatches a second and larger force, but cannot breach the fortifications. A typhoon ravishes the fleet and forces their retreat. Beginning of the myth that a "divine wind" (*kamikaze*) destroys Japan's enemies, that Japan is unique and inviolable.

1290   Nikkō founds Daiseki-ji Temple.

1333   Kamakura shogunate is destroyed.

1336–1392 Wars between rival imperial lines located in Yoshino and Kyoto, sometimes called the *Nanbokuchō* ("southern and northern dynasties") period. Ends when southern line agrees to return to Kyoto on condition that the throne alternate between the two lines (but the southern line never relinquishes the throne).

MUROMACHI OR ASHIKAGA PERIOD (1336–1573)

1338   Ashikaga Takauji is named *Seii-tai-shōgun* ("barbarian-subduing generalissimo") and establishes his shogunate in the Muromachi section of Kyoto.

c.1343 Kitabatake Chikafusa, a supporter of the southern

imperial line, writes the *Jinnō shōtōki* (Record of the legitimate succession of divine emperors), in which he maintains that Japan is unique and superior because of its unbroken line of divine rulers.

1436 Suppression of the Nichiren sect in Kamakura.

1457 Rennyo becomes eighth Chief Abbot of Hongan-ji Temple (True Pure Land sect).

1467 Outbreak of the decade-long Ōnin War (1467–1477), a battle over succession to the post of shogun that weakens shogunate control and leads to the period of warring states.

1474 First of a series of uprisings by True Pure Land sect followers in Kaga (area of present Ishikawa Prefecture).

1477 Beginning of the *sengoku jidai* or period of warring states (1477–1573).

1480 Uprisings by True Pure Land sect followers in many parts of the Hokuriku area.

1484 Yoshida Kanetomo establishes Yoshida Shinto.

1488 Peasant followers of the True Pure Land sect in the Kaga area foment a rebellion (*Kaga ikkō ikki*) and establish an autonomous government that survives for over a century.

1514 Shogunate suppresses True Pure Land sect in Harima (present-day Hyōgo Prefecture).

1521 True Pure Land sect is banned in Echigo province (now Niigata Prefecture).

n.d. Wang Yang-ming Neo-Confucianism introduced in late Muromachi period, possibly by Ryōan Keigo (1425–1514).

1543 Portuguese men, landing at Tanegashima, sell firearms (arquebuses) to the lord of the island, who has them reproduced and demonstrated to other military leaders.

1549 Christianity is formally introduced to Japan when Francis Xavier and two other Jesuits arrive in Kagoshima.

1560 Oda Nobunaga, through military prowess, becomes the most powerful daimyo and starts to eliminate rival powers, especially the military power of the Buddhist monasteries.

Shogun Ashikaga Yoshiteru gives permission to Portuguese Jesuit Gaspar Vilela to spread the Christian message.

1569   Oda Nobunaga gives permission to Spanish Dominican Luis Flores to reside in Kyoto and spread the Christian message.

1570–1580 Oda Nobunaga wages war against the True Pure Land sect, breaking its military power and taking possession of its Osaka fortress, Ishiyama Hongan-ji Temple.

1571   Oda Nobunaga razes 3,000 buildings in the compound of Enryaku-ji Temple and massacres most of its monks.

MOMOYAMA OR AZUCHI-MOMOYAMA PERIOD (1573–1603)

1576   At Azuchi, Oda Nobunaga builds a castle for his headquarters.

1580   English trading ships put in at Hirado.

1581   Oda Nobunaga puts to death over a thousand monks of Mt. Kōya, site of Kongōbu-ji, head temple of the Shingon sect.

1582   Oda Nobunaga is slain. Hideyoshi soon takes charge.

1583   Hideyoshi builds Osaka Castle. Tokugawa Ieyasu bans the True Pure Land sect in his domain.

1587   Hideyoshi issues edict banning all Christian missionaries and forbidding vassals to embrace Christianity without his permission. Edict is haphazardly enforced. With the protection of Christian daimyo, many missionaries go underground and continue to proselytize.

1588   Hideyoshi orders all peasants to surrender their swords and initiates a "sword hunt." Establishes visible class distinction between sword-bearing aristocrat and swordless commoner.

1589   Hideyoshi bans Christianity, razes Christian institutions in Kyoto.

1590   Hideyoshi's control over Japan becomes nearly complete.

Sen-no-Rikyū and others make the tea ceremony attractive to many.

1592   Hideyoshi invades Korea.

1594   For his headquarters, Hideyoshi builds a castle at Momoyama.

1596   A shipwrecked Spanish pilot boasts about colonial expansion. Hideyoshi suddenly enforces his ban on Christian missionaries.

1597   Hideyoshi has twenty-six Japanese and non-Japanese Christians crucified at Nagasaki.

1598   Hideyoshi dies. Rival daimyo compete for power.

1599   Franciscans begin missionary work in Edo.

1600   Tokugawa Ieyasu emerges as supreme power after victory at Sekigahara.

TOKUGAWA OR EDO PERIOD (1603–1868)

1603   Tokugawa Ieyasu is appointed *Seii-tai-shōgun* ("barbarian-subduing generalissimo") and establishes his shogunate at Edo (the present Tokyo).

1606   Ieyasu, though initially friendly to Christian missionaries, starts to issue anti-Christian edicts.

1608   Hayashi Razan becomes Confucian tutor to the Tokugawa shogun.

1608–1618   Regulations governing relationships between head and branch temples are instituted.

1612   Ieyasu orders all his Christian retainers to give up their religion. Some refuse and are executed. He starts to close down Christian churches.

1614   Ieyasu orders all Christian missionaries and prominent Japanese Christians deported, but many slip through his net.

1616   Ieyasu dies, and his son Hidetada, formally shogun since 1605, assumes power.

1617   Four Christian missionaries are executed.

1620   Nagasaki Commissioner destroys Christian churches and clinics.

1622   Execution of 120 Christian missionaries and Japanese believers.

Prohibition against construction of new Buddhist temples.

1629   At Nagasaki a plaque bearing the likeness of Christ or Mary is used as a test to identify suspected Christians. Those who refuse to tread on such a plaque (*fumie*) are tortured until they apostatize or die. This test spreads to other domains.

1632   Hidetada dies, and his son Iemitsu, formally shogun since 1623, assumes power.

1635   Shogunate establishes the office of Commissioner of Temples and Shrines (*Jisha Bugyō*). It also institutes the *sankin kōtai*, a system requiring daimyo to reside alternately in Edo and in their domains for a year at a time, leaving wives and children in Edo.

Approximate beginning of the *terauke seido*, a system requiring the priest of the local Buddhist temple to provide for every supporting household a written guarantee that each person named is affiliated with the temple and innocent of association with Christianity. Later combined with an annual *shūmon aratame* or "check on Buddhist sect affiliation." (The two together are called the *danka seido* or "system of temple-affiliated households.") In effect Buddhism becomes the established religion.

1637–1638   Shimabara Revolt, initially a peasant uprising against oppressive taxation, turns into a Christian rebellion. Nearly 20,000 men, plus women and children, are annihilated. Small pockets of clandestine Christians (*kakure kirishitan*) date from this time.

1641   Approximate beginning of Japan's two centuries of seclusion.

1646   Place of imprisonment for Christians is built in Edo.

1657   Work begins on the *Dai Nihon-shi* (History of great Japan) under the Mito school of Confucianism.

1778–1798   Motoori Norinaga publishes his *Kojikiden* (Commentary on the *Kojiki*).

1802   Kino establishes Nyoraikyō, harbinger of the "new religions."

1811   Hirata Atsutane, an anti-Buddhist, anti-Confucian Shinto restorationist whose ideas were temporarily influential in the early Meiji period (and again in the 1930s and early 1940s), publishes his *Kodō tai'i* (Threshold of the ancient way).

1814   Kurozumi Munetada founds Kurozumikyō.

1838   Nakayama Miki founds Tenrikyō.

1854   Commodore Matthew C. Perry of the U.S. demands a treaty. Japan emerges from seclusion; shogunate totters.

1859   Protestant and Roman Catholic missionaries reintroduce Christianity. Kawate Bunjirō founds Konkōkyō.

1861   Nicolai founds the Holy Orthodox Church in Japan.

1865   Petitjean's discovery of the clandestine Christians.

MODERN PERIOD (1868–)

MEIJI ERA (1868–1912)

1869   Meiji government disestablishes Buddhism and revives the ancient Department of Shinto Affairs (*Jingikan*).

1871   Climax of anti-Buddhist iconoclasm. Revocation of law establishing the *danka seido*. Iwakura Mission to the West.

1873   Removal of public notices proscribing Christianity.

1876   Japan "opens" Korea.

1877   Bureau of Shinto Shrines and Buddhist Temples (*Shaji Kyoku*) established in the Ministry of Home Affairs.

1889   Promulgation of the Meiji Constitution.

1890   Meiji Constitution goes into effect. Imperial Rescript on Education issued.

1891   Uchimura Kanzō provokes furor by refusing to bow before the Imperial Rescript on Education.

1892   Deguchi Nao founds Ōmoto.

1894–1895   Sino-Japanese War.

1900   Separate establishment of the Shrine Bureau (*Jinja Kyoku*) and the Religions Bureau (*Shūkyō Kyoku*).

1904–1905 Russo-Japanese War.

1910   Japan annexes Korea.

TAISHŌ PERIOD (1912–1925)

1913   Religions Bureau transferred from the Ministry of Home Affairs to the Ministry of Education.

1915–1920 World War I stimulates Japan's economy.

1923   Great earthquake in the Tokyo area.

1925   Peace Preservation Law. Kubo Kakutarō founds Reiyūkai.

SHŌWA PERIOD (1926–1988)

1929   Taniguchi Masaharu founds Seichō no Ie.

1930   Makiguchi Tsunesaburō begins Sōka Kyōiku Gakkai.

1931   Manchurian Incident.

1932   Religious education proscribed in public schools.

1937   Clash between Chinese and Japanese troops in the Beijing area leads to full-scale war.

1938   "New Order in East Asia" brings Manchuria and China under Japanese hegemony.

1939   Promulgation of Religious Organizations Law.

1940   Military expansion into Southeast Asia in order to establish the "Greater East Asia Co-Prosperity Sphere" (*Dai tōa kyōeiken*).

1941   Establishment of the United Church of Christ in Japan.
       Attack on Pearl Harbor and consequent enlargement of the Pacific War.

1945   End of World War II and beginning of Allied Occupation. Land reform. Abrogation of the Peace Preservation Law, the Religious Organizations Law, etc. Issuance of the Shinto Directive and the Religious Juridical Persons Ordinance.

1946   Emperor formally rejects the idea that he is a kami.
       Establishment of the Jinja Honchō (Association of Shinto Shrines).

Promulgation of the Constitution of Japan.

1947   Constitution of Japan goes into effect.
New family law written into the Civil Code, abolishing the traditional family system.

1948   Diet pronounces Imperial Rescript on Education invalid.
Formal establishment of the Korean Christian Church in Japan.

1951   Religious Juridical Persons Law replaces Religious Juridical Persons Ordinance.
San Francisco Peace Treaty and United States–Japan Security Treaty are signed.
Establishment of the *Shin Nihon Shūkyō Dantai Rengōkai* (Union of New Religious Organizations of Japan).

1952   Allied Occupation ends. San Francisco Peace Treaty and United States–Japan Security Treaty go into effect.

1960   Kagawa Toyohiko dies (age 71).

1963   Government sponsors at Yasukuni Shrine a requiem service for fallen military personnel.

1964   Sōka Gakkai sponsors establishment of the Kōmeitō (Clean Government Party).

1965   Emperor and empress, on October 19, attend a ritual at Yasukuni Shrine in commemoration of the twentieth anniversary of the end of World War II. One day later the Nihon Izoku Kai (Bereaved Society of Japan) sponsors, at Yasukuni Shrine, the first *senbotsusha ireisai* (Shinto rite for the repose of the spirits of military personnel who died for emperor and country).

1966   Suzuki Daisetz dies (age 95).

1967   A bill to support Yasukuni Shrine with public funds arouses strong reactions.

1968   Intensification of anti-establishment political action by university students throughout Japan.

1969   The bill to support Yasukuni Shrine with public funds goes to the Diet; Buddhist and Christian bodies issue protests.

The Association of Shinto Shrines launches the Shintō Seiji Renmei (League for Shinto Politics). 47 Kōmeitō candidates elected to House of Representatives.

1970   Sōka Gakkai announces its revocation of *shakubuku,* a browbeating conversion technique. Kōmeitō announces its decision to act independently of Sōka Gakkai.

1971   Okinawa reverts to Japan, and Okinawan religious organizations originally incorporated under the Religious Organizations Law of 1939, together with Shinto shrines registered in the official register of Shinto shrines (*Jinja Meisaichō*), are recognized as religious juridical persons under the Religious Juridical Persons Law of 1951.

1974   The Liberal-Democratic Party's bill to support Yasukuni Shrine with public funds passes in the House of Representatives but fails in the House of Councilors.

1977   Supreme Court, ruling on the Tsu City case, decides it is not unconstitutional for a government organization to sponsor a Shinto *jichinsai,* or grounds-purification rite.

1978   Tōjō Hideki (1884–1948), wartime Minister of War, Chief of Staff, and head of the Ministry of Munitions, later convicted and executed by the International Military Tribunal for the Far East as a war criminal, is enshrined with other Class A war criminals at Yasukuni Shrine.

1979   Matsuoka Yōsuke (1880–1946), former Foreign Minister and architect of the Japan-Germany-Italy tripartite axis alliance, is enshrined at Yamaguchi Gokoku Shrine.
        Promulgation of the law requiring all institutions that serve the public to date all documents with the *gengō* (era name and year) connected with the Japanese emperor.

1981   Pope John Paul II visits Japan, meets with emperor, makes peace appeal in Hiroshima, traces path of Christian martyrs in Nagasaki.

1985   Nakasone Yasuhiro participates in Shinto rites at Yasukuni Shrine in his official capacity as prime minister. Angry reactions from neighboring countries, especially China and South Korea.

1988   Supreme Court rules that the Self-Defense Forces did not violate the Constitution in the enshrinement of deceased officer Nakaya Takafumi, and that even if it had engaged in religious activity, the state is not to be held accountable unless coercion can be proved.

1989   Emperor Hirohito dies January 7. Henceforth to be known as Emperor Shōwa. Crown Prince Akihito succeeds him. Heisei period begins.

HEISEI PERIOD (1989–)

1990   In completion of the succession process for Emperor Akihito, the Sokui-no-rei enthronement ceremony is held on November 12. The nightlong Daijōsai ("Great Food Offering Ceremony"), widely reported as a Shinto rite in which the new emperor assumes divine character, is held from the evening of November 22.

Bibliography

ABE Yoshiya 阿部美哉. "Religious Freedom under the Meiji Constitution." *Contemporary Religions in Japan* 9 (1968): 268–338 (and serially in the next five issues of this journal).

—————. "From Prohibition to Toleration: Japanese Government Views Regarding Christianity, 1854–73." *Japanese Journal of Religious Studies* 5 (1978): 107–38.

ABRAHAMS, Roger D. and Richard BAUMAN. "Ranges of Festival Behavior." In Barbara A. BABCOCK, ed., *The Reversible World: Symbolic Inversion in Art and Society*. Ithaca: Cornell University Press, 1978.

AISAWA Hisashi 相沢 久. *Kokka to shūkyō* 国家と宗教 [State and religion]. Tokyo: Daisan Bunmeisha, 1977.

AKAIKE Noriaki 赤池憲昭. "Sympathetic Understanding and Objective Observation." *Japanese Journal of Religious Studies* 9 (1982): 53–64.

ANDREWS, A. A. *The Teachings Essential for Rebirth: A Study of Genshin's Ōjōyōshū*. Tokyo: Sophia University, 1973.

ANESAKI Masaharu 柿崎正治. *History of Japanese Religion*. London: Kegan Paul, 1930; Rutland, Vermont and Tokyo: Charles E. Tuttle, 1963.

ARAKI Michio 荒木美智雄. "Toward an Integrated Understanding of Religion and Society: Hidden Premises in the Scientific Apparatus of the Study of Religion." *Japanese Journal of Religious Studies* 9 (1982): 65–76.

ARUGA Kizaemon 有賀喜左衛門. "Kazoku no kokusai hikaku" 家族の国際比較 [An international comparison of the family]. In *Aruga Kizaemon chosaku shū* 有賀喜左衛門著作集 [Collected works of Aruga Kizaemon] (Tokyo: Miraisha, 1970), 9: 155–220.

BATESON, Gregory. *Naven: A Survey of the Problems Suggested by a Composite Picture of the Culture of a New Guinea Tribe Drawn from Three Points of View*, 2nd ed. Stanford, California: Stanford University Press, 1958.

_____. *Steps to an Ecology of Mind*. San Francisco: Chandler Publications, 1970.

BECKFORD, James and Thomas LUCKMANN, eds. *The Changing Face of Religion*. London: Sage, 1989.

BELLAH, Robert N. *Tokugawa Religion: The Values of Pre-industrial Japan*. Glencoe, Illinois: Free Press, 1957.

_____. *Beyond Belief: Essays on Religion in a Post-traditional World*. New York: Harper and Row, 1970.

BELLAH, Robert N., ed. *Religion and Progress in Modern Asia*. New York: Free Press, 1965.

BERGER, Peter L. *The Sacred Canopy: Elements of a Sociological Theory of Religion*. Garden City, New York: Doubleday, 1967.

BERGER, Peter L. and Thomas LUCKMANN. *The Social Construction of Reality: A Treatise in the Sociology of Knowledge*. Garden City, New York: Doubleday Anchor Books, 1966.

BERMAN, Morris. *The Reenchantment of the World*. Toronto and New York: Bantam Books, 1981.

BERTHIER-CAILLET, L. *Fêtes et rites des quatre saisons au Japon*. Paris: Publications Orientalistes de France, 1981.

BLACKER, Carmen. *The Catalpa Bow: A Study of Shamanistic Practices in Japan*. London: Allen & Unwin; Totowa, New Jersey: Rowman, 1975.

BROWN, Norman O. *Love's Body*. New York: Alfred A. Knopf and Random House, 1966.

Bukkyō Bunka Kenkyūkai仏教文化研究会, ed. *Butsuji no shikitari* 仏事のしきたり [Proper behavior at Buddhist ceremonies]. Osaka: Hikari no Kuni, 1976.

_____. *Senzo kuyō* 先祖供養 [Services for the repose of the ancestors]. Osaka: Hikari no Kuni, 1977.

Bunkachō 文化庁 [Agency for Cultural Affairs, Ministry of Education]. *Meiji ikō shūkyō seido hyakunen shi* 明治以降宗教制度百年史 [Religious organizations during the hundred years since Meiji]. Tokyo: Bunkachō, 1970.

CALDAROLA, Carlo. *Christianity: The Japanese Way.* Leiden: Brill, 1979.

CARY, Otis. *A History of Christianity in Japan: Roman Catholic, Greek Orthodox, and Protestant Missions,* 2 vols. Rutland, Vermont and Tokyo, Japan: Charles E. Tuttle, 1976. First publ. 1909.

COLCUTT, Martin. *Five Mountains: The Rinzai Zen Monastic Institution in Medieval Japan.* Cambridge, Massachusetts: Council on East Asian Studies, Harvard University, 1981.

CREEMERS, W. H. M. *Shrine Shinto after World War II.* Leiden: Brill, 1968.

DAVIS, W. B. *Dojo: Magic and Exorcism in Modern Japan.* Stanford, California: Stanford University Press, 1980.

DOERNER, David L. "Comparative Analysis of Life after Death: Folk Shinto and Christianity." *Japanese Journal of Religious Studies* 4 (1977): 151–82.

DOUGLAS, Mary. *Purity and Danger: An Analysis of the Concepts of Pollution and Taboo.* London: Routledge and Kegan Paul, 1966.

_____. *Natural Symbols: Explorations in Cosmology.* New York: Random House, 1970, 1973.

_____. *Implicit Meanings: Essays in Anthropology.* London: Routledge and Kegan Paul, 1975.

DRUMMOND, Richard H. *A History of Christianity in Japan.* Grand Rapids, Michigan: Eerdmans, 1971.

EARHART, H. Byron. "Gedatsukai: One Life History and Its Significance for Interpreting Japanese New Religions." *Japanese Journal of Religious Studies* 7 (1980): 227–57.

_____. *Japanese Religion: Unity and Diversity,* 3rd ed. Belmont, California: Wadsworth, 1982.

_____. *Gedatsu-kai and Religion in Contemporary Japan: Returning to the Center.* Bloomington, Indiana: Indiana University Press, 1989.

ELIOT, Charles. *Japanese Buddhism.* London: Routledge; New York: Barnes and Noble, 1959. First publ. 1935.

FENN, Richard K. "The Secularization of Values: An Analytical Framework for the Study of Secularization." *Journal for the Scientific Study of Religion* 8 (1969): 112–24.

FUJII Masao 藤井正雄. *Gendaijin no shinkō kōzō* 現代人の信仰構造 [The faith-structure of modern Japanese people] . Tokyo: Hyōronsha, 1974.

————. "Gendaijin no shūkyō kōdō" 現代人の宗教行動 [The religious behavior of contemporary Japanese people]. *Jurisuto*, no. 21 (1981): 132–38.

FUJIWARA Hirotatsu 藤原弘達. *Sōka Gakkai o kiru* 創価学会を斬る [Beheading Sōka Gakkai]. Tokyo: Nisshin Hōdō, 1969.

————. *Zoku Sōka Gakkai o kiru* 続・創価学会を斬る [Sequel to beheading Sōka Gakkai]. Tokyo: Nisshin Hōdō, 1971.

FURUNO Kiyoto 古野清人. *Kakure kirishitan* 隠れキリシタン [Underground Christians]. Tokyo: Shibundō, 1959.

————. "Kirishitanizumu no hikaku kenkyū" キリシタニズムの比較研究 [A comparative study of Christian syncretism]. In *Furuno Kiyoto chosaku shū* 古野清人著作集 [Collected works of Furuno Kiyoto], vol. 5. Tokyo: San'ichi Shobō, 1973.

GEERTZ, Clifford. *The Interpretation of Cultures.* New York: Basic Books, 1973.

GLACKEN, Clarence J. *The Great Loochoo: A Study of Okinawan Village Life.* Berkeley and Los Angeles: University of California Press, 1955; Rutland, Vermont and Tokyo, Japan: Charles E. Tuttle, 1960.

GLASER, Barney G. and Anselm L. STRAUSS. *The Discovery of Grounded Theory: Strategies for Qualitative Research.* New York: Aldine de Gruyter, 1967.

GLOCK, Charles Y. and Rodney STARK. *Religion and Society in Tension.* Chicago: Rand McNally, 1965.

HANAYAMA Shōyū 花山勝友. *Sōshiki, hōyō, nipponkyō* 葬式・法要・日本教 [Funerals, Buddhist rites, and the religion of being Japanese]. Tokyo: Fujin Seikatsusha, 1975.

HARDACRE, Helen. *Lay Buddhism in Contemporary Japan: Reiyūkai Kyōdan.* Princeton: Princeton University Press, 1984.

_____. *Shintō and the State, 1868–1988*. Princeton: Princeton University Press, 1989.

HASHIMOTO, Tatsumi. *Ancestor Worship and Japanese Daily Life*, transl. by Percy T. Luke. Tokyo: Word of Life Press, 1962.

HERTZ, Robert. "A Contribution to the Study of the Collective Representation of Death." In *Death and the Right Hand*, transl. by Rodney and Claudia Needham. Glencoe, Illinois: The Free Press, 1960. First publ. as "Contribution à une étude sur la représentation collective de la mort" (1907).

HIRAI Naofusa 平井直房. "Shinto." *Encyclopaedia Britannica*, 15th ed., *Macropaedia*, vol. 16. Chicago: Encyclopaedia Britannica, 1982.

HORI Ichirō 堀一郎. *Folk Religion in Japan: Continuity and Change*. Chicago: University of Chicago Press; Tokyo: University of Tokyo Press, 1968.

_____. "Shamanism in Japan," transl. by David Reid. *Japanese Journal of Religious Studies* 2 (1975): 231–87.

_____. "Japanese Religion." *Encyclopaedia Britannica*, 15th ed., *Macropaedia*, vol. 10. Chicago: Encyclopaedia Britannica, 1982.

HORI Ichirō et al., eds. *Japanese Religion: A Survey by the Agency for Cultural Affairs*, transl. by Abe Yoshiya and David Reid. Tokyo and Palo Alto, California: Kodansha International, 1972.

HOZUMI Nobushige 穂積陳重. *Ancestor-Worship and Japanese Law*, 2nd and rev. ed. Tokyo: Maruzen, 1912.

HUNTINGTON, Richard and Peter METCALF. *Celebrations of Death: The Anthropology of Mortuary Ritual*. Cambridge: Cambridge University Press, 1979.

HUSSERL, Edmund. *The Crisis of European Sciences and Transcendental Phenomenology*, transl. by David Carr. Evanston, Illinois: Northwestern University Press, 1970. First publ. as *Die Krisis der europäischen Wissenschaften und die transzendentale Phänomenologie* (1936).

IKADO Fujio 井門富二夫. "The Origin of the Social Status of Protestant Christianity in Japan (1859–1918)" (1st half). *Contemporary Religions in Japan* 2/1 (1961): 1–29.

_____. "The Origin of the Social Status of Protestant Christianity in

Japan (1859–1918)" (2nd half). *Contemporary Religions in Japan* 2/2 (1961): 30–68.

_____. *Sezoku shakai no shūkyō* 世俗社会の宗教 [Religion in a secular society]. Tokyo: Nihon Kirisuto Kyōdan Shuppan Kyoku, 1972.

IKEDA Daisaku 池田大作. *Seiji to shūkyō* 政治と宗教 [Politics and religion]. Tokyo: Otori Shoin, 1964.

_____. *Seiji to shūkyō* [Politics and religion], rev. ed. Tokyo: Ushio Shuppansha, 1969.

INOKUCHI Shōji 井之口章次. *Nihon no sōshiki* 日本の葬式 [The Japanese funeral]. Tokyo: Chikuma Shobō, 1977.

Japan Statistical Yearbook. Tokyo: Nihon Tōkei Kyōkai, 1989.

INOUE Nobutaka 井上順孝 et al. *Shin shūkyō kenkyū chōsa handobukku* 新宗教研究調査ハンドブック [Research and survey handbook on the new religions]. Tokyo: Yūsankaku Shuppan, 1981.

KASAHARA Kazuo 笠原一男, ed. *Nihon shūkyōshi* 日本宗教史 [A history of Japanese religion], vol. 2. Tokyo: Yamakawa Shuppansha, 1977.

KAWAWATA Yuiken 河和田唯賢. "Religious Organizations in Japanese Law." In HORI Ichirō et al., eds., *Japanese Religion* (1972): 161–70.

Kirisutokyō nenkan 基督教年鑑 [Yearbook on Christianity]. Tokyo: Kirisuto Shinbunsha, 1968, 1969, 1970, 1971, 1972.

KISHIMOTO, Hideo 岸本英夫. *Shūkyōgaku* 宗教学 [Religious studies]. Tokyo: Taimeidō, 1961.

KITAGAWA, Joseph M. *Religion in Japanese History.* New York: Columbia University Press, 1966.

KOIKE Kenji 小池健治, NISHIKAWA Shigenori 西川重則, and MURAKAMI Shigeyoshi 村上重良, eds. *Shūkyō dan'atsu o kataru* 宗教弾圧を語る [Conversations about religious persecution]. Tokyo: Iwanami Shoten, 1978.

KŌMOTO Mitsugu 孝本 貢. "Gendai toshi no minzoku shinkō — Kakyō saiken to chinkon" 現代都市の民俗信仰―家郷再建と鎮魂 [Folk religion in the modern city: Relocating the family home and the repose of souls]. In ŌMURA and NISHIYAMA, eds., *Gendaijin no shūkyō* [The religion of present-day people] (1988): 33–75.

KUWABARA Shigeo 桑原重夫. "Nihon Kirisuto Kyōdan no naibu kokuhatsu" 日本基督教団の内部告発 [Internal indictment of the United Church of Christ in Japan]. *Gendai no me* 19/3 (1978): 88–95.

LEBRA, Takie Sugiyama. *Japanese Patterns of Behavior*. Honolulu: University Press of Hawaii, 1976.

———. "Ancestral Influence on the Suffering of Descendants in a Japanese Cult." In William H. NEWELL, ed., *Ancestors*. The Hague: Mouton, 1976.

LEBRA, William P. *Okinawan Religion: Belief, Ritual, and Social Structure*. Honolulu: University of Hawaii Press, 1966.

LUCKMANN, Thomas. *The Invisible Religion: The Problem of Religion in Modern Society*. New York: Macmillan, 1967.

———. "Theories of Religion and Social Change." *Annual Review of the Social Sciences of Religion* 1 (1977): 1–27.

———. *Life-World and Social Realities*. London: Heinemann Educational Books, 1983.

MACÉ, François. "The Funerals of the Japanese Emperors." *Bulletin of the Nanzan Institute for Religion and Culture* 13 (1989): 26–37.

MALINOWSKI, Bronislaw. *The Dynamics of Culture Change*. New Haven: Yale University Press, 1945.

MARTIN, David. *The Religious and the Secular: Studies in Secularization*. London: Routledge and Kegan Paul, 1969.

———. *A General Theory of Secularization*. Oxford: Basil Blackwell, 1978.

MATSUMOTO Shigeru 松本 滋 . *Motoori Norinaga: 1730–1801*. Cambridge, Massachusetts: Harvard University Press, 1970.

MATSUNO Junkō 松野純孝. "Buddhist Sects." In HORI Ichirō et al., eds., *Japanese Religion* (1972): 191–213.

MATSUO Yoshiyuki 松尾義行 . "Sengo hoshu seiji to shūkyō kyōdan" 戦後保守政治と宗教教団 [Postwar conservative politics and religious organizations]. *Gendai no me* 19/3 (1978): 62–71.

MCMULLIN, Neil. "Historical and Historiographical Issues in the Study of Pre-modern Japanese Religions." *Japanese Journal of Religious Studies* 16 (1989): 3–40.

MELAND, Bernard Eugene. *The Secularization of Modern Cultures*. New York: Oxford University Press, 1966.

MIYAKE Hitoshi 宮家 準 . *Shugendō girei no kenkyū* 修験道儀礼の研究 [Studies in Shugendō ritual], revised and enlarged ed. Tokyo: Shunjūsha, 1985.

————. *Shugendō shisō no kenkyū* 修験道思想の研究 [Studies in Shugendō thought]. Tokyo: Shunjūsha, 1985.

————. *Shugendō jiten* 修験道辞典 [Shugendō dictionary]. Tokyo: Tōkyōdō Shuppan, 1986.

MORIOKA Kiyomi 森岡清美 . "Nihon nōson ni okeru kirisutokyō no juyō" 日本農村における基督教の受容 [Reception of Christianity in a Japanese rural community]. In *Kindai shisō no keisei* 近代思想の形成 [The development of modern thought], rev. ed., 193–240. Tokyo: Ochanomizu Shobō, 1959.

————. *Shinshū kyōdan to "ie" seido* 真宗教団と「家」制度 [The Shinshū Buddhist orders and the *ie* system] . Tokyo: Sōbunsha, 1962.

————. *Nihon no kindai shakai to kirisutokyō* 日本の近代社会とキリスト教 [Modern Japanese society and Christianity]. Tokyo: Hyōronsha, 1970.

————. *Religion in Changing Japanese Society.* Tokyo: University of Tokyo Press, 1975.

————. *Ie no henbō to senzo no matsuri* 家の変貌と先祖の祭 [The transformation of the household and the rites for ancestors]. Tokyo: Nihon Kirisuto Kyōdan Shuppan Kyoku, 1984.

MORIOKA Kiyomi and William H. NEWELL, eds. *The Sociology of Japanese Religion.* Leiden: Brill, 1968.

MUNAKATA Iwao 宗像 厳 . "The Ambivalent Effects of Modernization on the Traditional Folk Religion of Japan." *Japanese Journal of Religious Studies* 3 (1976): 99–126.

MURAKAMI Shigeyoshi 村上重良 . *Nihon hyakunen no shūkyō — Haibutsu kishaku kara Sōka Gakkai made* 日本百年の宗教—排仏毀釈から創価学会まで [A hundred years of religion in Japan: From anti-Buddhist iconoclasm to Sōka Gakkai]. Tokyo: Kōdansha, 1968.

————. *Gendai shūkyō to seiji* 現代宗教と政治 [Present-day religion and politics]. Tokyo: Tokyo Daigaku Shuppankai, 1978.

————. *Shin shūkyō* 新宗教 [New religions]. Tokyo: Hyōronsha, 1980.

———. *Japanese Religion in the Modern Century*, transl. by H. Byron Earhart. Tokyo: University of Tokyo Press, 1980.

NAKAMAKI Hirochika 中牧弘充 . "Continuity and Change: Funeral Customs in Modern Japan." *Japanese Journal of Religious Studies* 13 (1986): 177–92.

NAKAMURA Hajime 中村 元 . *Ways of Thinking of Eastern Peoples: India, China, Tibet, Japan*, rev. English transl., ed. by P. P. Wiener. Honolulu: East-West Center Press, 1964.

———. "Japanese Philosophy." *Encyclopaedia Britannica*, 15th ed., *Macropaedia*, vol. 10. Chicago: Encyclopaedia Britannica, 1982.

NATANSON, Maurice, ed. *Phenomenology and Social Reality: Essays in Memory of Alfred Schutz*. The Hague: Martinus Nijhoff, 1970.

NEWELL, William H., ed. *Ancestors*. The Hague: Mouton, 1976.

———. "Good and Bad Ancestors." In William H. NEWELL, ed., *Ancestors*. The Hague: Mouton, 1976.

NHK Yoron Chōsabu NHK 世論調査部 , ed. *Nihonjin no shūkyō ishiki* 日本人の宗教意識 [The religious consciousness of the Japanese people]. Tokyo: Nippon Hōsō Shuppan Kyōkai, 1984.

Nichiren Shōshū yōgi 日蓮正宗要義 [Essential teachings of the Nichiren Shōshū]. Fujinomiya: Nichiren Shōshū Shūmuin, 1978.

Nihon shūkyō jiten 日本宗教事典 [Dictionary of Japanese Religions]. ONO Yasuhiro 小野泰博 et al., eds. Tokyo: Kōbundō, 1985.

NISHIKAWA Shigenori 西川重則 . "The Daijōsai, the Constitution, and Christian Faith." *Japan Christian Quarterly* 56 (1990): 132–46.

NORBECK, Edward. *Religion and Society in Modern Japan: Continuity and Change*. Houston, Texas: Tourmaline Press, 1970.

OBATA Susumu 小畑 進 . *Kirisutokyō keichōgaku jiten—Kon to sō* キリス ト教敬弔学辞典—婚と葬 [A Christian handbook for joyful and sad occasions: Weddings and funerals]. Tokyo: Inochi no Kotoba Sha, 1978.

OFFNER, Clark. "Continuing Concern for the Departed." *Japanese Religions* 11 (1979): 1–16.

OGAWA Keiji 小川圭治, ed. *Nihonjin to kirisutokyō* 日本人とキリスト教 [The Japanese and Christianity]. Tokyo: Sanseidō, 1973.

OGUCHI Iichi 小口偉一 and HORI Ichirō 堀 一郎, eds. *Shūkyōgaku jiten*

宗教学辞典 [Dictionary of religious studies]. Tokyo: Tokyo Daigaku Shuppankai, 1973.

ŌMURA Eishō 大村英昭 and NISHIYAMA Shigeru 西山 茂, eds. *Gendaijin no shūkyō* 現代人の宗教 [The religion of present-day people]. Tokyo: Yūhikaku, 1988.

OOMS, Herman. "The Religion of the Household: A Case Study of Ancestor Worship in Japan." *Contemporary Religions in Japan* 8 (1967): 201–333.

————. "A Structural Analysis of Japanese Ancestral Rites and Beliefs." In William H. NEWELL, ed., *Ancestors*. The Hague: Mouton, 1976.

PARKER, F. Calvin. *Jonathan Goble of Japan: Marine, Missionary, Maverick*. Lanham, Maryland: University Press of America, 1990.

PARSONS, Talcott. *The System of Modern Societies*. Englewood Cliffs, New Jersey: Prentice-Hall, Inc., 1971.

PIERIS, Aloysius. *An Asian Theology of Liberation*. Maryknoll, New York: Orbis Books, 1988.

PLATH, David W. "Where the Family of God is the Family: The Role of the Dead in Japanese Households." *American Anthropologist* 66 (1964): 300–17.

RABINOW, Paul. *Reflections on Fieldwork in Morocco*. Berkeley and Los Angeles: University of California Press, 1977.

RABINOW, Paul and William M. SULLIVAN, eds. *Interpretive Social Science: A Reader*. Berkeley: University of California Press, 1979.

READER, Ian. "The Rise of a Japanese 'New New Religion': Themes in the Development of Agonshū." *Japanese Journal of Religious Studies* 15 (1988): 235–61.

REID, David. "Shōyu kusai kirisutokyō" 醤油くさいキリスト教 [A Christianity that reeks of soy sauce]. *Asoka*, no. 133 (1973): 23–27.

————. "Kōzōshugi" 構造主義 [Structuralism]. In OGUCHI and HORI, *Shūkyōgaku jiten* [Dictionary of religious studies] (1973), 193–96.

————. "Reflections: A Response to Professors Yanagawa and Abe." *Japanese Journal of Religious Studies* 10 (1983): 309–15.

————. "Amerikajin no seishikan: Pyūritan no sōsō girei o chūshin ni" アメリカ人の生死観―ピューリタンの葬送儀礼を中心に [American views of life and death: Focus on Puritan mortuary rites]. *Kirisuto Shinbun*, nos. 2091–99 (1988).

REID, David, MATSUMOTO Shigeru 松本 滋 , SUZUKI Norihisa鈴木範久, and Jan SWYNGEDOUW . *Kiku to katana to jūjika to* 菊と刀と十字架と [The chrysanthemum, the sword, and the cross]. Tokyo: Nihon Kirisuto Kyōdan Shuppan Kyoku, 1976.

REISCHAUER, Edwin 0. *The Japanese*. Cambridge, Massachusetts: Belknap Press of Harvard University Press, 1977.

ROTERMUND, H. 0. *Die Yamabushi: Aspekte ihres Glaubens, Lebens und ihrer sozialen Funktion im japanischen Mittelalter*. Hamburg: Cram & De Gruyter, 1968.

SCHUTZ, Alfred. *Collected Papers I: The Problem of Social Reality*, ed. by Maurice NATANSON. The Hague: Martinus Nijhoff, 1962.

————. *The Phenomenology of the Social World*, transl. by George Walsh and Frederick Lehnert. London: Heinemann Educational Books, 1967.

————. *Collected Papers II: Studies in Social Theory*, ed. by Arvid BRODERSEN. The Hague: Martinus Nijhoff, 1976.

————. *Collected Papers III: Studies in Phenomenological Philosophy*, ed. by I. SCHUTZ. The Hague: Martinus Nijhoff, 1975.

SHIBATA Chizuo. "Christianity and Japanese Ancestor Worship Considered as a Basic Cultural Form." *Northeast Asia Journal of Theology*, nos. 22–23 (1979): 62–71.

SHIMAZONO Susumu 島薗 進 . "The Living Kami Idea in the New Religions of Japan." *Japanese Journal of Religious Studies* 6 (1979): 389–412.

————. "The Development of Millennialistic Thought in Japan's New Religions: From Tenrikyō to Honmichi." In James A. BECKFORD, ed., *New Religious Movements and Rapid Social Change*. London: Sage, 1986.

————. "Conversion Stories and their Popularization in Japan's New Religions." *Japanese Journal of Religious Studies* 13 (1986): 157–75.

SHINER, Larry. "The Concept of Secularization in Empirical Research." *Journal for the Scientific Study of Religion* 6 (1967): 207–20.

SHINOHARA Kōichi. "Religion and Political Order in Nichiren's Buddhism." *Japanese Journal of Religious Studies* 8 (1981): 225–35.

Shinshūkyō jiten 新宗教事典 [Dictionary of new religions]. INOUE Nobutaka 井上順孝 et al., eds. Tokyo: Kōbundō, 1990.

Shugendo and Mountain Religion in Japan. *Japanese Journal of Religious Studies* 16 (1989): 93–256.

Shūkyō nenkan 宗教年鑑 [Religions yearbook]. Tokyo: Bunkachō, 1978 and succeeding years through 1990.

SMITH, Robert J. *Ancestor Worship in Contemporary Japan.* Stanford, California: Stanford University Press, 1974.

————. "Who are the 'Ancestors' in Japan? A 1963 Census of Memorial Tablets." In William H. NEWELL, ed., *Ancestors.* The Hague: Mouton, 1976.

SMITH, Warren W., Jr. *Confucianism in Modern Japan: A Study of Conservatism in Japanese Intellectual History,* 2nd ed. Tokyo: Hokuseido Press, 1973.

Sōka Gakkai no rinen to jissen 創価学会の理念と実践 [Sōka Gakkai in ideal and practice]. Tokyo Daigaku Hokekyō Kenkyūkai, ed. Tokyo: Daisan Bunmeisha, 1975.

SONODA Minoru 薗田 稔. "The Traditional Festival in Urban Society." *Japanese Journal of Religious Studies* 2 (1975): 103–36.

SPAE, Joseph J. *Itō Jinsai: A Philosopher, Educator and Sinologist of the Tokugawa Period.* New York: Paragon Book Reprint, 1967. First publ. 1948.

SUGIMOTO, Masayoshi and David L. SWAIN. *Science and Culture in Traditional Japan: A.D. 600–1854.* Cambridge, Massachusetts: MIT Press, 1978; Rutland, Vermont and Tokyo, Japan: Charles E. Tuttle, 1989.

SWYNGEDOUW, Jan. "Sezokuka" 世俗化 [Secularization]. In OGUCHI and HORI, eds., *Shūkyōgaku jiten* [Dictionary of religious studies] (1973), 495–97.

————. "Secularization in a Japanese Context." *Japanese Journal of Religious Studies* 3 (1976): 283–306.

————. "A Rejoinder." *Japanese Journal of Religious Studies* 5 (1978): 28–32.

_____. "Japanese Religiosity in an Age of Internationalization." *Japanese Journal of Religious Studies* 5 (1978): 87–106.

_____. "Japanese Religions and Party Politics: Some Recent Examples." *Japan Missionary Bulletin* 32 (1978): 541–49.

TAKAKUSU Junjirō. *The Essentials of Buddhist Philosophy*, 2nd ed., W. T. CHAN and C. A. MOORE, eds. Honolulu: University of Hawaii, 1949.

TAKEDA Chōshū 竹田聴洲 . *Sosen sūhai — Minzoku to rekishi* 祖先崇拝 — 民俗と歴史 [Ancestor worship: Ethnology and history]. Kyoto: Heirakuji Shoten, 1957.

_____. "Sosen sūhai — Nihon" 祖先崇拝 — 日本 [Ancestor worship — Japan]. In OGUCHI and HORI, eds., *Shūkyōgaku jiten* [Dictionary of religious studies] (1973), 514–16.

_____. *Nihonjin no "ie" to shūkyō* 日本人の「家」と宗教 [The Japanese "household" and religion]. Tokyo: Hyōronsha, 1976.

TAMAKI Hajime玉城 肇. "Nihon no kazoku: Seido to jittai no rekishi" 日本の家族 — 制度と実体の歴史 [The Japanese family: A history of its structure and actual condition]. *Jurisuto*, no. 6 (1977): 30–40.

TAMARU Noriyoshi 田丸徳善. "'Sezokuka' gainen ni kansuru oboegaki" 「世俗化」概念に関する覚書 [A memorandum on the concept of "secularization"]. In WAKIMOTO Tsuneya, ed., *Shakai henkaku to shūkyō* [Social change and religion]. Privately distributed, 1978.

TAMARU Noriyoshi, ed. *Gendai tennō to shintō* 現代天皇と神道 [The emperor and Shinto today]. Tokyo: Tokuma Shoten, 1990.

TANAKA Hisao 田中久夫. *Sosen saishi no kenkyū* 祖先祭祀の研究 [Ancestral rite studies]. Tokyo: Kōbundō , 1978.

THOMAS, Winburn T. *Protestant Beginnings in Japan: The First Three Decades, 1859–1889*. Rutland, Vermont and Tokyo, Japan: Charles E. Tuttle, 1959.

TYLER, Stephen A. *Cognitive Anthropology*. New York: Holt, Rinehart and Winston, 1969.

VAN GENNEP, Arnold. *The Rites of Passage*, transl. by Monika B. Vizedom and Gabrielle L. Caffee. Chicago: University of Chicago Press, 1960. First publ. as *Les rites de passage* (1908).

WAKIMOTO Tsuneya 脇本平也 . "Shūkyōgaku" 宗教学 [Religious studies]. In OGUCHI and HORI, eds., *Shūkyōgaku jiten* [Dictionary of religious studies] (1973), 267–74.

WAKIMOTO Tsuneya, ed. *Shakai henkaku to shūkyō o meguru shomondai* 社会改革と宗教をめぐる諸問題 [Problems concerning social change and religion]. Privately distributed, 1978.

WATANABE Shōkō 渡辺照宏. *Nihon no bukkyō* 日本の仏教 [Japanese Buddhism]. Tokyo: Iwanami Shoten, 1958.

WHITE, James W. *The Sokagakkai and Mass Society*. Stanford, California: Stanford University Press, 1970.

WILSON, Bryan. *Contemporary Transformations of Religion*. London: Oxford University Press, 1976.

————. "Aspects of Secularization in the West." *Japanese Journal of Religious Studies* 3 (1976): 259–76.

————. "The Functions of Religion in Contemporary Society." (A lecture delivered in Tokyo on January 17, 1979.)

WOODARD, William P. *The Allied Occupation of Japan 1945–1952 and Japanese Religions*. Leiden: E. J. Brill, 1972.

YAMAUCHI Rokurō 山内六郎. *Kirisutokyō kankon sōsai nyūmon* キリスト教冠婚葬祭入門 [A Christian introduction to rites of passage]. Tokyo: Seibunsha, 1973.

YANAGAWA Keiichi 柳川啓一. "Theological and Scientific Thinking about Festivals," transl. by David Reid and Jan Swyngedouw. *Japanese Journal of Religious Studies* 1 (1974): 5–49.

YANAGAWA Keiichi, ed. *Gendai shakai to shūkyō* 現代社会と宗教 [Modern society and religion]. Tokyo: Tōyō Tetsugaku Kenkyūsho, 1978.

————, ed. *Seminā shūkyōgaku kōgi* セミナー宗教学講義 [A seminar concerning (Professor Yanagawa's) lectures on religious studies]. Kyoto: Hōzōkan, 1988.

YANAGAWA Keiichi and ABE Yoshiya. "Some Observations on the Sociology of Religion in Japan." *Actes [de la] 14ème Conférence Internationale de Sociologie Religieuse* (Lille: C.I.S.R.) as reprinted in the *Japanese Journal of Religious Studies* 5 (1978): 5–27.

————. "Reply." *Japanese Journal of Religious Studies* 5 (1978): 33–36.

————. "Cross-cultural Implications of a Behavioral Response." *Japanese Journal of Religious Studies* 10 (1983): 289–307.

_____. *Shūkyō riron to shūkyōshi* 宗教理論と宗教史 [Theory of religion and history of religions]. Tokyo: Nihon Hōsō Shuppan Kyōkai, 1985.

YANAGITA Kunio 柳田國男. "Senzo no hanashi" 先祖の話 [The story of our ancestors]. In *Teihon Yanagita Kunio shū* 定本柳田國男集 [Definitive edition of the collected works of Yanagita Kunio] (Tokyo: Iwanami Shoten, 1962), 10: 1–152. In English as *About our Ancestors*, transl. by Fanny Hagin Mayer and Ishiwara Yasuyo. Tokyo: Ministry of Education, 1970.

YINGER, Milton J. *Religion, Society and the Individual: An Introduction to the Sociology of Religion*. New York: Macmillan, 1957.

_____. *The Scientific Study of Religion*. New York: Macmillan, 1970.

YONEMURA Shōji. "*Dōzoku* and Ancestor Worship in Japan." In William H. NEWELL, ed., *Ancestors*. The Hague: Mouton, 1976.

Index and Glossary

Birth 26. *See also* Rites, of passage
Bon 盆 festival 24–25, 106, 110 n.,
111, 115, 131–32, 148, 154. *See
also* Festivals
BROWN, Norman O. 66 & n.
Buddha altar (*butsudan*). *See also*
Buddhism, and buddha altar;
Kami altar; mortuary tablet
absence of 102, 129
association with death and ancestors 22, 104, 125
as basis for analysis of change in
Protestant Christianity 125,
130, 133
and belief in Buddhist 130–31
disposal of, by first Christians
110
and grave visits 141 n., 143
household possession of 113,
114, 125, 126, 129
and memorial photo 103, 114,
115 n., 135, 137, 140, 147 & n.
practices before 125, 137–39
and religious objects in home
133–36
and ritual process 27, 105–106,
110 n., 113, 114, 131–32, 139
and shrine visits 141 n., 144 & n.
and tangible benefits, prayer for
141 n., 143–44
Buddha, becoming a living (*sokushin
jōbutsu*) 14 & n., 16
Buddhahood, attribution of, to the
dead 14 n.
Buddha nature 17
Buddha's birthday 23.
Buddhism. *See also* Religion; State
religion
adherents to 7, 28
and buddha altar 126, 130–31
and common people 19
and *danka seido* 10
and death 27, 106
growth of 7, 28
introduction of 8–10
lay associations of
Honmon Butsuryūshū 13, 14,
27– 28

Reiyūkai 13, 25 n., 28–29
Risshō Kōseikai 13, 28–29
Sōka Gakkai 13, 28, 46
modification of 98 & n.
Nichiren 18, 46, 48
and political power 8, 10, 14, 15,
35 & n., 49 n., 77–78
Pure Land 17
Shingon 17
and Shinto 8, 19
and Shugendō 10–11
Tantric 17
Tendai 8, 10, 16, 17, 43, 155
and *terauke seido* 10, 162
True Pure Land 17
Zen. *See* Zen Buddhism
Buppō minshū 仏法民衆 (one people
under the Buddhist law) 49
Bureau of Shinto Shrines and Bud-
dhist Temples (*Shaji Kyoku*) 36 n.,
163
Burial. *See also* Funeral; Mortuary
rites
double 99 , 103
final 105
Butsudan 仏壇 . *See* Buddha altar
Byakkō Shinkōkai 白光真宏会 30 & n.

Catholics, Japanese 98, 121 n.
Change, religions 15–16, 19, 31–
32
Child, newborn, to Shinto shrine
142, 144 & n.
Chopsticks, at crematorium 104
Christianity. *See also* Catholics,
Japanese; Missionaries, Nation-
building; Protestantism, Japanese
adherents to 7, 28
and ancestral cult tradition 97–
98 & n., 108–9, 112, 118
and death 107–8, 111
and dual religious affiliation 114
and emperor system 92
and Expo 83
growth of 7, 28
and "idol worship" 109, 112
influence of 57, 78–79, 110

NAKASONE Yasuhiro 中曽根康弘 44, 49–51, 50 n., 55, 166. *See also* Court cases
NAKAYA Takafumi 中谷孝文 52, 167
NAKAYA Yasuko 中谷康子 52, 54
Nakaya case 52–54, 55. *See also* Court cases
NATANSON, Maurice 66 & n.
Nation building, as motive for conversion to Christianity 80 n. *See also* Conversion
Natural community 34, 37, 55, 58. *See also* Community
Neo-Confucianism 12, 18–19, 157, 159. *See also* Confucianism
New Year (*shōgatsu*) 22–24, 105 & n., 147. *See also* Festivals
New religions 27–31
 founding of 12, 13, 16, 27, 163, 164
 growth of 27–28
 influence of Nichiren teachings in 18
 of magic and miracle 30–31
 in modernization stream 27–30
 and neglected ancestral spirits 25 n.
 in "Other" class 7 n.
 reasons people join 29–30, 31
 and Sect Shinto 14 n.
 of Shinto tradition 14
 Shugendō ideas and practices in 14
 size of 13
 types of 14–15
 union of 47 n., 165
Nichiren 日蓮 (1222–1282) 18, 28, 46, 157–58. *See also Lotus Sūtra*; Nichiren Shōshū; Sōka Gakkai
Nichiren Shōshū 日蓮正宗 28, 41, 43, 46, 48–49
Nihon Kirisuto Kyōdan 日本基督教団 (United Church of Christ in Japan) 38, 46, 71–72, 75, 80, 93, 95–96, 112, 121 & n., 164
NIIJIMA Jō 新島襄 (1843–1890) 109–10, 117
Nodobotoke 喉仏 (Adam's apple) 104.

See also Cremation
Norms, conflict of 33–34, 37, 89, 93
Nyorai 如来 12
Nyoraikyō 如来教 12 n., 13, 14 n. 163

Objectivity 62
Ōbutsu myōgō 王仏冥合 (fusion of imperial authority and Nichiren Buddhism) 46
ODA Nobunaga 織田信長 (1534–1582 10, 159–60
Offerings 22, 52 n., 114, 139–40. *See also* Religious behavior
Ōharai 大祓 (grand purification) 23. *See also* Festivals
Okuribi 送り火 (a fire to see ancestral spirits off) 106. *See also* Fire; *Mukaebi*
Oya 親 (parent) 45, 116, 122
Oyakata 親方 (person in a parental role) 116
Oya kyōkai 親教会 (parent church) 116

Participant-observer 63
Participation by representation 34
Peace 30, 38 n., 80 n.
Peace Preservation Law 164
Period of warring states (*sengoku jidai*, 1477–1573) 19, 159
Persecution, religious 14 n., 15, 41, 79 & n., 159
Pharisees 119–20, 149
Photograph, of the deceased 103, 114, 115 n. *See also* Memorial photos
Polarization 81–83, 87, 89–90, 92
Political orientation 144–46, 148 n.
Politico-religious unity (*saisei itchi*) 35–39, 41–42, 46. *See also* Religiosity; Religious freedom; Religious groups
Population 7, 20–22, 24
 growth 7, 9
 mobility 76, 102, 113
 religious 21–22
Positivism 62

Protestantism, Japanese 97–99, 111–13, 115–16, 118
Public juridical persons 38 n.
Pure Land (*jōdo*) 8, 10, 17
Pure Land Sect (Jōdo Shū) 17–18, 43, 156–57. *See also* True Pure Land Sect
Puritan mentality 122, 149
Purity of heart 5, 18, 94

RABINOW, Paul 66 & n.
Rebirth 16. *See also* Buddha, becoming a living
REDFIELD, Robert 4
Reinōsha 霊能者 (spiritualist medium) 30
Reiyūkai 霊友会 13, 25 n., 28–29, 43, 164
Religion. *See also* Buddhism; Christianity; New Religions; Religious groups; Shinto
  cosmic 4–6
  definitions of 37, 55, 65, 144 n.
  folk 3, 30, 144 n.
  majority 120–21
  metacosmic 4–5, 6
  minority 15, 120
  secular 73–74
  Shinto, as exception to idea of 37, 40, 42, 45, 55, 78, 80 n., 144 n.
  traditional 77–78
Religion and state 33–34. *See also* Frame
  anti-traditional unity model 41–44, 49, 54–56
  separation model 39–40, 41–42
  traditional unity model 41, 44, 46, 54–58
Religiosity
  community 34–35, 36, 37, 39, 55, 58
  individual 34–35, 37, 39, 55, 58
Religions Bureau (*Shūkyō Kyoku*) 37, 164
Religious affiliation 114
Religious behavior 3, 114, 141–44. *See also* Offerings; Religious practices

Religious bodies, illegal 79. *See also* Legal recognition
Religious change 15–16, 19–31–32. *See also* Modernization; Secularization
Religious developments 16, 19, 31
Religious freedom. *See also* Court cases; Law; Religion and state; Religiosity
  coercion and 51, 54, 55, 167
  Constitution and 27, 32, 36, 39, 41
  denial of, by Nichiren Shōshū 28
  establishment of, in Constitution (1947) 27, 32, 39, 41
  establishment of, in Meiji Constitution (1890) 36, 41, 80 n.
  institutionalization of 37
  law implementing 40
  offset by Imperial Rescript on Education (1890) 36
  scope of 37–38, 41, 51, 53
  and separation of religion and state (*seikyō bunri*) 27, 32, 39–41, 40 n., 54, 55, 167
  Sōka Gakkai and 49 n.
  violation of 38, 40, 54
Religious groups
  anti-traditional unity class 41–44, 49, 54–56
  Japanese 41
  separation of religion and state class 41–42, 43, 44, 51, 54–55, 56–58
  traditional unity class 41–42, 43, 44, 46, 54–57, 58
Religious Juridical Persons Law (*Shūkyō hōjin hō*) 40–41, 40 n., 165–66
Religious Juridical Persons Ordinance (*Shūkyō hōjin rei*) 40 n., 164–65
Religious leaders, premodern 16–19
Religious objects in home 133–36. *See also* Mortuary tablet
Religious Organizations Law